Noël Coward was born in Teddington, Middlesex on 16 December 1899. His professional acting career began in 1911 and in 1918 he wrote the first of his plays which was subsequently to be staged. He created a sensation as playwright and actor with *The Vortex* in 1924 and followed through with *Hay Fever* and *Easy Virtue* in 1925 and the operette *Bitter-Sweet* in 1929, for which he wrote book, music and lyrics as well as directing. His *Private Lives* in 1930 launched the stage partnership with Gertrude Lawrence which was renewed later in the thirties with *Tonight at 8.30*. *Cavalcade, Design for Living* and an autobiography, *Present Indicative*, were the other high-points of this decade. In the early forties *Blithe Spirit* was produced in London and Coward himself toured playing the lead in this and in *Present Laughter* and *This Happy Breed* for six months in 1942/3. He also wrote, acted in, produced and co-directed the film *In Which We Serve*. The forties also saw the films *Blithe Spirit* and *Brief Encounter*. In the fifties Coward began a new career as a cabaret entertainer as well as writing *Relative Values*, *Quadrille* and *Nude With Violin* and publishing *Future Indefinite*, a second volume of autobiography. He left England and moved first to Bermuda and then to Switzerland. In the sixties he turned novelist with *Pomp and Circumstance* and published his *Collected Short Stories* and a book of verse, *Not Yet the Dodo*. His play *Waiting in the Wings* was produced together with the musicals *Sail Away* and *The Girl Who Came to Supper*. He acted his last stage role in his *Suite in Three Keys* in 1966. He was knighted in 1970 and died in Jamaica on 26 March 1973.

The front cover painting by Noël Coward is reproduced by kind permission of The Noël Coward Estate.

BOOKS BY NOËL COWARD

*published by Methuen, London
†published by Methuen, Inc, New York

Noël Coward

COLLECTED VERSE

Edited by
Graham Payn and Martin Tickner

A Methuen Paperback

This collection first published in Great Britain in 1984
by Methuen London Ltd, 11 New Fetter Lane, London EC4P 4EE
and in the United States of America in 1985
by Methuen Inc, 29 West 35th Street, NY1001
Corrected paperback edition first published in 1987

Some of the verses in this volume were previously published
in *Not Yet The Dodo* by Noël Coward. For details see Index.

The Noël Coward lyrics quoted at the beginning of each section
are included in *The Lyrics of Noël Coward*
re-issued by Methuen London in 1983
and copyright © the Estate of the late Noël Coward

Photoset in 10 point Garamond by ⮝Tek-Art, Croydon, Surrey
Printed in Great-Britain by
Richard Clay Ltd, Bungay, Suffolk

British Library Cataloguing in Publication Data

Coward, Noël
  Collected verse.
  I. Title II. Payn, Graham   III. Tickner, Martin
  821'.912   PR6005.085

  ISBN 0 413 551504

Contents

WAR . . . AND PEACE

TRAVEL . . . AND TRAVELLERS

Introduction

"Throughout most of the years of my life, since approximately nineteen hundred and eight, I have derived a considerable amount of private pleasure from writing verse."

It was with these words that Noël Coward began the introduction to his previously published book of verse, *Not Yet The Dodo*, in 1967. From Noël's Diaries it is apparent that most of the verse included in that earlier volume was written specially for it:

"I find it quite fascinating to write at random, sometimes in rhyme, sometimes not. I am trying to discipline myself away from too much discipline, by which I mean that my experience and training in lyric writing has made me inclined to stick too closely to a rigid form. It is strange that technical accuracy should occasionally banish magic, but it does. The carefully rhymed verses, which I find very difficult not to do, are, on the whole, less effective and certainly less moving than the free ones. This writing of free verse, which I am enjoying so very much, is wonderful exercise for my mind and for my vocabulary. Most of what I have already done I really feel is good and is opening up, for me, some new windows. My sense of words, a natural gift, is becoming more trained and selective, and I suspect, when I next sit down to write a play, things may happen that have never happened before."

Not Yet The Dodo contained twenty-six verses ("less than a quarter of my total output"). This new collection contains eighty – not only everything in *Dodo* but fifty-four more verses, most of which have never appeared in print before. What we have here is virtually all the verse Noël wrote which is suitable for publication. All that is left out are the parodies he prepared under other names for

Spangled Unicorn and *Chelsea Buns*, which have mostly been republished anyway.

In addition, certain private "correspondence" has been omitted. As Noël put it: "I have automatically enjoyed verse as a means of communication with my intimates ever since I can remember. Lorn Loraine, my beloved secretary and English representative for forty-six years, is an expert at squeezing the maximum of business information and personal news into rhymed cables and telegrams which, together with my also rhymed replies, has afforded us both a lot of amusement. The amusement however is private and too esoteric to interest anyone apart from ourselves. Many of the communications exchanged would be completely unintelligible to the lay reader. Additionally, I once churned out a few cheerful little couplets riding on a camel in the Sahara desert which, so far as I can remember, were too obscene to be preserved for posterity. As however they happened to be blown away in a sandstorm they may after all be preserved for posterity and be discovered centuries hence like the Dead Sea Scrolls. As they were unsigned I hereby seize the opportunity of publicly disowning them."

During the original preparation of the present collection a letter appeared in a London newspaper commenting on the Memorial Stone to Noël in Westminster Abbey. The writer felt that it was quite wrong for Noël to be commemorated in 'Poet's Corner' as he was not a poet. Of course he wasn't and never pretended to be. The Stone in Westminster Abbey is not in Poet's Corner but in what is becoming known as 'Actors' Aisle'. Noël wrote 'verse' not 'poetry' and certainly never saw himself as the Byron or Tennyson of his generation.

Of verse-writing he said, "It is an inherent instinct in the English character. it is surprising how many unexpected, non-literary minds take to verse at the slightest encouragement. In the Services for instance, particularly the Royal Navy, at least on the bridges and in the wardrooms where I have so frequently been a guest, the scribbling of doggerel to highlight some specific event or situation is an accepted routine. There are few admirals, captains and commanders who have not, at some time or other, dispatched rhymed couplets via their 'Signals' operators to their opposite numbers in adjacent ships. In fact verse and apt quotations from the Bible are sent whizzing back and forth as a matter of course. These are occasionally obscene, always pertinent and usually extremely witty. Whether or not the officers of other Navies indulge in this brain-teasing little game I do not know, but I doubt it, it is such a typically British brand of irreverent flippancy."

The verse contained in this collection whether funny, serious, angry or witty simply goes to prove what countless admirers of Noël's work have always known. That to the lasting soubriquet hung on him quoted from his own *Bitter Sweet* – "a talent to amuse" can be added "and in particular a talent to *entertain*".

The final comment must be Noël's: "I truly love writing both rhymed and unrhymed verse. It's complicated and exasperating but rewarding when it comes off."

Readers should note that a number of minor alterations have been made to this edition of *The Collected Verse* from that originally published in 1984.

Graham Payn and Martin Tickner
Winter 1986

LOVE
LIFE . . . AND DEATH

LOVE

"Time and tide can never sever
Those whom love has bound for ever,
Dear Lover of my Dreams come true"

Cavalcade

I am No Good at Love

I am no good at love
My heart should be wise and free
I kill the unfortunate golden goose
Whoever it may be
With over-articulate tenderness
And too much intensity.

I am no good at love
I batter it out of shape
Suspicion tears at my sleepless mind
And, gibbering like an ape,
I lie alone in the endless dark
Knowing there's no escape

I am no good at love
When my easy heart I yield
Wild words come tumbling from my mouth
Which should have stayed concealed;
And my jealousy turns a bed of bliss
Into a battlefield.

I am no good at love
I betray it with little sins
For I feel the misery of the end
In the moment that it begins
And the bitterness of the last good-bye
Is the bitterness that wins.

This is
to Let You Know

This is to let you know
That there was no moon last night
And that the tide was high
And that on the broken horizon glimmered the lights of
    ships
Twenty at least, like a sedate procession passing by.

This is to let you know
That when I'd turned out the lamp
And in the dark I lay
That suddenly piercing loneliness, like a knife,
Twisted my heart, for you were such a long long way
    away.

This is to let you know
That there are no English words
That ever could explain
How, quite without warning, lovingly you were here
Holding me close, smoothing away the idiotic pain.

This is to let you know
That all that I feel for you
Can never wholly go.
I love you and miss you, even two hours away,
With all my heart. This is to let you know.

I Knew You
Without Enchantment

I knew you without enchantment
And for some years
We went our usual ways
Meeting occasionally
Finding no heights nor depths among our days
Shedding no tears
Every so often when we felt inclined
Lying like lovers in each other's arms
Feeling no qualms
In our light intimacy
So resolute we were in heart and mind
So steeled against illusion, deaf and blind
To all presentiment, to all enchantment
(I knew you without enchantment).

It is so strange
Remembering that phase
Those unexacting, uneventful days
Before the change
Before we knew this serio-comic, tragic
Most unexpected, overwhelming magic.
I knew you without enchantment.

And to-day I cannot think of you without my heart
Suddenly stopping
Or, in those long grey hours we spent apart
Dropping, dropping
Down into desolation like a stone.
To be alone
No longer means to me clear time and space
In which to stretch my mind.

I see your face
Between me and the space I used to find
Between me and the other worlds I seek
There stands your sleek
And most beloved silhouette
And yet
I can remember not so long ago
We neither of us cared
Nor dared
To know
How swiftly we were nearing the abyss
(This foolish, quite ungovernable bliss)
Let's not regret
That empty life before. It was great fun
And hurt no one
There was no harm in it
At certain moments there was even charm in it.

But oh my dearest love, there was no spell
No singing heaven and no wailing hell.
I knew you without enchantment.

Morning Glory

'There's something rather sad' she said
'In seeing a great big ship go down'
She languidly shook her lovely head
And plucked the edge of the eiderdown.
Her hands were white and her nails were red
Her marble brow wore a pensive frown
'It's really terribly sad' she said
'To see a beautiful ship go down'
The breakfast tray lay across her knee
A dusty beam of sunlight shone
On fruit and silver and China tea
And a crumbled, half-devoured scone.
The thin blue smoke of her cigarette
Wove, above us, a tangled skein,
The end of it, where her lips had met,
Proudly boasted a scarlet stain.
As though appalled by her own surmise
She gave a shudder and then a stretch
And turned her empty, lambent eyes
To have a look at the *Daily Sketch*.
The front page headlines were large and black
The pictures under them blotched, obscene
A few dark heads in the swirling wrack
'Survivors' stories on page sixteen'
She read a little and sipped her tea
'Fifty passengers safe and sound'
Then she brightened perceptibly
'Fourteen hundred and fifty drowned'
She read the glutinous journalese
That smeared the names of the lost and dead
Then, rather neatly, controlled a sneeze

'That was sheer agony' she said
I looked at the lissom, graceful line
Her body made 'neath the silken sheet
Her heart so far so far from mine
Yet I could almost hear it beat.
I wandered back over hours of sleep
To try to catch at the night gone by
To see if morning would let me keep
At least a fragment of memory.

Honeymoon. 1905.

'They were married
And lived happily ever after.'
But before living happily ever after
They drove to Paddington Station
Where, acutely embarrassed, harassed
And harried;
Bruised by excessive jubilation
And suffering from strain
They got into a train
And, having settled themselves in a reserved carriage,
Sought relief, with jokes and nervous laughter,
From the sudden, frightening awareness of their marriage.

Caught in the web their fate had spun
They watched the suburbs sliding by,
Rows of small houses, neatly matched,
Safe, respectable, semi-detached;
Lines of gardens like pale green stripes,
Men in shirtsleeves smoking pipes
Making the most of a watery sun
In a watery English sky.

Then pollard willows and the river curving
Between high trees and under low grey bridges
Flowing through busy locks, looping and swerving
Past formal gardens bright with daffodils.
Further away the unpretentious hills
Rising in gentle, misty ridges,
Quiet, insular, and proud
Under their canopies of cloud.

Presently the silence between them broke,
Edward, tremulous in his new tweed suit
And Lavinia, pale beneath her violet toque,
Opened the picnic-basket, lovingly packed
By loving hands only this morning – No!
Those sardine sandwiches were neatly stacked
Lost centuries ago.
The pale, cold chicken, hard-boiled eggs and fruit
The cheese and biscuits and Madeira cake
Were all assembled in another life
Before 'I now pronounce you man and wife'
Had torn two sleepers suddenly awake
From all that hitherto had been a dream
And cruelly hurled
Both of them, shivering, into this sweeping stream
This alien, mutual unfamiliar world.

A little later, fortified by champagne
They sat, relaxed but disinclined to talk
Feeling the changing rhythms of the train
Bearing them onward through West Country towns
Outside in the half light, serene and still,
They saw the fading Somersetshire Downs
And, gleaming on the side of a smooth, long hill
A white horse carved in chalk.

Later still, in a flurry of rain
They arrived at their destination
And with panic gripping their hearts again
They drove from the noisy station
To a bright, impersonal double room
In the best hotel in Ilfracombe.

They opened the window and stared outside
At the outline of a curving bay,
At dark cliffs crouching in the spray
And wet sand bared by the falling tide.
The scudding clouds and the rain-furrowed sea
Mocked at their desperate chastity.
Inside the room the gas globes shed,
Contemptuous of their bridal night,

A hard, implacable yellow light
On a hard, implacable double bed.

The fluted mahogany looking-glass
Reflecting their prison of blazing brass,
Crude, unendurable, unkind.
And then, quite suddenly, with a blind
Instinctive gesture of loving grace,
She lifted her hand and touched his face.

Reunion

'It's lovely to have you back' she said
But the tone was pitched too high
He, sitting opposite, crumbled a roll
Made like a crescent with black seeds on it,
Lit a cigarette and tried to smile;
A gesture devastating in its hopelessness,
A gallant effort, gallantly designed
To reassure her, an abortive, brave attempt
To cut at least a temporary clearing
In the surrounding jungle. She smiled back
Seeing him, for an instant, suddenly
Clearly and vividly as he once had been
Before the cruel, separating years
Had altered everything. She turned away
And fumbled in her bag to hide her tears.
Outside the open window, light summer rain
Had left a sheen on the Soho street
Reflecting stars and moon and neon lights
At the feet of stranger characters
Shuffling back and forth, pausing at corners
To whisper in alien tongues and then retire
Back into the shadows.
Inside the restaurant the customers sat
Encased in impersonal, synthetic cosiness
There were small red lamps on all the tables
And rather untidy vases of anemones,
Whenever the service door swung open
There was a smell of garlic and frying fat
And the noise of banging crockery in the kitchen.
When the Maître d'Hôtel brought the menu
The atmosphere eased a little

14

Because there was something to say.
He was sallow and swarthy, the Maître d'Hôtel,
With sadness in his chocolate-coloured eyes,
Suddenly she longed to catch at his coat tails and cry
(In Italian of course) 'Cheer up – cheer up
You'll be going home some day
Home to your own place, your own familiar unhygienic
    village
With the olive groves rolling up to the sky
And the Campanile and the Piazza
Where the people you really know pass by'
But he took their order and went away
And at their table the silence lay
And the evening stretched before them
Bleak, desolate and grey
With so much so much so much to think
And so little, so little to say.

LIFE

"I believe that since my life began
The most I've ever had is just
A talent to amuse."

Bitter Sweet

Not Yet the Dodo

In the countryside of England
Tucked snugly beneath the Sussex Downs
Or perhaps a mile or two away
From gentle cathedral towns
There still exist to-day
A diminishing few
A residue
Of unregenerate characters who
Despite two wars and the Welfare State
And incomes sadly inadequate
Still, summoned by Sunday morning chimes,
Walk briskly to church to say their prayers
And later, in faded chintz arm-chairs,
Read of divorces, wars and crimes
And, shocked by the trend of world affairs,
Compose,
In a cosy, post-prandial doze,
Tart letters of protest to *The Times*.
These people still tap the weather-glass
And prune their roses and mow their grass
Representative
For so long as they live
Of the English upper middle-class.

General and Lady Bedrington
Lived on the borders of Cornwall and Devon
In a red-brick, weather-bleached Georgian house
With a distant view of the sea,
They drove into Plymouth twice a week
In an ancient Austin Seven
And in summer, on rather a sloping lawn,

Played croquet after tea,
The thirty years of their married life
Had been lived in far away places,
Before and during and after the war
They'd always been on the move.
Alien climates and tropical suns
Had sallowed their English faces
And now, at long last, their elderly ways
Were set in a tranquil groove.
The household staff which should have been six
Was reduced to one and a 'daily'.
The 'one' was Maggie Macdonald
Who'd been Lady Bedrington's maid
In the early, hurly-burly days
When they'd settled themselves so gaily
In that 'barracky' house in the compound
Of the Garrison at Port Said.
Later, when Priscilla was born
And so sadly and swiftly died,
It was Maggie who coped with everything,
Efficient beyond belief.
It was Maggie who, in the desolate hours,
Stayed by her mistress' side
And with dour, stubborn Scottish sense
Blunted the edges of grief.

It was Maggie also who, some years after,
When Barry was born in Delhi,
Nursed Lady B through the merciless heat
And ultimately contrived,
On a breathless morning at six o'clock,
While the bugles were sounding Reveille,
To deliver the baby an hour and a half
Before the doctor arrived.

And later still, when war had come,
She brought the boy home to his Granny
In a crowded troopship that sailed for England
Under a brazen sky.
She fluttered a handkerchief from the deck,
Proud of her role as a 'Nanny',

While Lady Bedrington, blinded with tears,
Waved the convoy 'good-bye'.

Maggie Macdonald was old and grey
But far from full of sleep
She had rheumatism in hip and knee
And her eyes were not what they used to be
But she woke with the morning every day
As though she'd a tryst to keep.

She ran the house like an oiled machine,
She did the marketing, cooked the meals:
On afternoons off, in her Sunday black
She walked three miles to the village and back
With a vast, asthmatical Aberdeen
Lumbering at her heels.

Maggie saw no indignity
In the fact that she worked for others.
She returned to Scotland once a year
For a fortnight's family atmosphere
In a little grey house outside Dundee
With one of her married brothers.

There were lots of relatives, brusque but kind;
Grandnephews and nieces to see
She brought them presents and gave them treats
And walked with them through the Dundee streets
But always, at the back of her mind,
Where the General and Lady B.

But even more than the Bedringtons
It was Barry who claimed her heart,
She wept each time he left for school,
Upbraiding herself for a doting fool
And stuffed him with cream and saffron buns
And apple and blackberry tart.

And when, as an undergraduate,
He came home for long week-ends,
She washed his shirts and pressed his slacks

And lied for him and covered his tracks
And was ready with soda-bi-carbonate
For him and his Oxford friends.

The problem of Barry's future career
Blew up at his coming-of-age.
He chose his moment and seized his chance
And, in the library after the dance
Announced, in a voice quite firm and clear,
That he meant to go on the stage.

The General went purple in the face,
Lady Bedrington kept her head.
They both of them tried to talk him round
But the boy inflexibly held his ground
Until at last, with unhappy grace,
They surrendered and went to bed.

Maggie was told the news the next day
And felt she might easily faint
But she pursed her lips and packed his bags,
Gloomily tied on the luggage tags
And waved the pride of her life away
To his world of powder and paint.

General and Lady Bedrington
With inward excitement but outward calm
Arrived, as usual, at Paddington
Where Barry was waiting, efficient and kind,
Though the General noticed, with vague alarm,
That his hair was rather too long behind.
With him was standing a tall young man
Wearing corduroys and an open sweater
Who, Barry explained, was Danny Hoag
With whom he was sharing a two-room flat
In a cul-de-sac off the Earl's Court Road.
He added, impressively, that Dan
Quite frequently drew designs for *Vogue*
And Lady B, with a private sigh,
Ardently wished she could like him better.
Barry procured a cab outside

And off they drove through the London rain
Danny dripping with Irish charm,
Caressing them with his gentle brogue
Barry, voluble, chatting away,
Telling them with self-conscious pride,
About the theatre, about the play,
About some pompous old Blimp who wrote
Explosively to the *Telegraph*
Protesting against the author's use
Of four-letter words and his abuse
Of England's quality, England's pride
England's achievements past and present.
The General stared at the street outside
And thought the play sounded damned unpleasant.

When they had reached the De Glenn hotel
And the boys had taken the taxi on,
General and Lady Bedrington,
After their welcome from the staff,
Walked upstairs to their double room
Both thinking thoughts best left unsaid
Both of them trying valiantly,
Sitting together on the bed,
To help each other to vanquish gloom.
'I didn't think much of that Irish bloke!'
The General murmured unhappily.
His wife, as though he had made a joke,
Laughed indulgently, patted his knee
And telephoned down to order tea.

They went to the theatre
Sat through the play
And were shocked, bewildered and bored,
And, during the final curtain calls,
Numb, in their complimentary stalls,
They looked at each other, looked away
And forced themselves to applaud.

The audience straggled up the aisle
And vanished into the mews
But both the General and Lady B,

Frozen in hopeless apathy
Sat on in silence for a while
Like people who've had bad news.

Stunned, inarticulate and deeply tired
They finally were led resignedly
Up four steep steps and through an iron door
To meet the cast and author of the play.
The odd young woman who escorted them
Wore, with a skin-tight jumper, denim slacks,
Black stockings, grubby plimsolls and a beret
From under which curtains of greasy hair
Descended to her shoulders. On the stage
Barry received them and presenting them
With filial pride and touching eagerness,
To all his strange colleagues who stood around
Proudly upon their consecrated ground.
Poor Lady Bedrington, with social grace,
Managed to conquer her embarrassment
And murmer some polite but empty phrases.
The General, mute before his only son,
Finally cleared his throat and said, 'Well done!'

The supper party after the play
In Barry and Danny's flat
Could not be accurately called
An unqualified success.
The cast were all invited
And some other cronies appeared
Including a sibilant gentleman
In velvet slacks and a beard
And a sullen Lesbian in evening dress
Who brought a Siamese cat.

General and Lady B were received
With cautious politesse.
A tall girl offered them sandwiches
And a whisky and soda each.
They sat on a sofa side by side
And longed to be home in bed.
There was little ham in the sandwiches

And a great deal too much bread
But they chewed them bravely, bereft of speech,
Encased in self-consciousness.

The party, after an hour or two,
Abandoned its formal endeavour.
A sallow youth with enormous ears
Was coaxed to do imitations.
The people he mimic'd obviously
Were known to everyone there
But the Bedringtons rather missed the point
For they didn't know who they were
And Barry's hissed explanations
Bewildered them more than ever.

A girl with slightly projecting teeth
Agreed, after much persuasion,
To tell the story of how she'd been
Seduced in 'digs' in Hull.
The present company evidently
Had heard it often before
And when she'd finished, vociferously,
Demanded an encore
To which she at once assented
And told an equally dull,
Long, complicated anecdote
Which was even more Rabelaisian.

The Bedringtons, over their married years,
Had learned to accept defeats.
So, at the same moment, they both got up
Still smiling with frozen eyes.
A hush descended upon the group
While politenesses were said
And Lady Bedrington's cloak was fetched
From Barry and Danny's bed.
Barry got them a taxi
And, muttering swift 'good-byes'
They drove back to the De Glenn hotel
Through the bright, deserted streets.

That night they lay, restless, in their thin twin beds
And Lady B discreetly wept a little.
The General, equally wretched, bravely tried
To reassure her, soothe her with platitudes.
'Youth will be served,' he said, 'We can't expect
Old heads on young shoulders, this is a passing phase,
He'll soon grow out of it. Cheer up my dear,
It's dangerous to take up moral attitudes.
Let the young idiot and his ghastly friends
Enjoy themselves and go their foolish ways.'
He got out of his bed to kiss her cheek
As he had done for nearly forty years.
'Silly old thing,' she said, and dried her tears.
The General, having got back to bed,
Switched off the light and, turning on his side,
Tried, unsuccessfully to sleep.
Lady B also, in the oppressive dark,
Waited unhopefully for oblivion.
Again, entirely soundlessly, she wept
Again it was almost dawn before they slept.

The royal garden parties every year
Vast numbers of loyal subjects are invited.
From South and West and East and North they come,
Some from the country, some from the suburbs, some
(On leave from Zanzibar or the Seychelles)
From inexpensive Kensington hotels.
Matriarchs in large hats and flowered prints,
Ebony delegates from far Dominions,
One or two sharp-eyed ladies from the Press,
Tiny green gentlemen in native dress,
Colonial Governors with eager wives
Jostling in line for when the Queen arrives.
Bright debutantes quite recently presented,
Actresses of impeccable repute,
A novelist or two, bishops galore,
Plus members of the diplomatic corps,
A smattering of ancient admirals
And matrons from the London hospitals.
Cabinet ministers, some rural deans,
Newly created knights and peers and Dames,

Field-marshals, air marshals, a few V.C.s.
Sauntering beneath the royal trees
Every mutation of the middle-class
Proudly parading on the royal grass.

The Queen, surrounded by her retinue,
Graciously moves among her varied guests.
Curtseys are made, heads are correctly bowed
And as she makes her progress through the crowd
Pauses are organized for conversation
With those marked on the list for presentation.
Following her, forming their separate groups,
Some other members of the royal family,
Sharing with affable, polite mobility,
Part of the afternoon's responsibility.
After an hour or so of this routine,
Either in blazing sun or gentle rain,
The royalties, by mutual consent,
Withdraw themselves to an exclusive tent,
Weary of bobbing head and bended knee,
And thankfully sit down to have their tea.

The porter at the De Glenn hotel
Having procured a hired limousine,
Stood to attention as the Bedringtons
Set proudly forth to keep their regal tryst.
The General, in top hat and morning-coat,
Lady B, in a floating chiffon dress,
Climbed with unhurried calm into the car
Though Lady B's enormous cartwheel hat
Needed to be manoeuvered with some care.
Walter, the valet, Rose, the chambermaid,
Ernest, the waiter on the second floor,
Waved from the landing window, while Miss Holt,
Her pince-nez glinting in the morning sun,
Forsook the cashier's desk and with a cry,
Rushed down the hotel steps to say 'good-bye'.

We British are a peculiar breed
Undemonstrative on the whole.
It takes a very big shock indeed

To dent our maddening self-control.

The slow decline of our Island Race
Alien prophets have long foreseen,
But still, to symbolize English grace,
We go to London to see the Queen.

Our far-flung Empire imposed new rules
And lasted a century or so
Until, engrossed with our football pools
We shrugged our shoulders and let it go.

But old traditions are hard to kill
However battered about they've been.
And it's still, for some, an authentic thrill
To go to London to see the Queen.

The car moved very slowly through the traffic.
Its occupants sat still, preserving elegance,
The General would liked to have crossed his legs
And smoked a cigarette, but he refrained;
His trousers were well-pressed and must remain
Well-pressed until he got back home again.

Sense of Occasion and the Royal touch
Wakened in their reactionary hearts
Old memories of less disturbing years
When social values were more specified.
Before the proletariat, en masse,
Reversed the status of the ruling class.

For them the afternoon (until the end)
Was beautiful and somehow reassuring.
They saw the Queen pass by and Lady B
Executed a most successful curtsey:
Then the Queen Mother, with her lovely smile,
Chatted to them both for quite a while.

Past friends appeared, perhaps a little changed:
Emily Blake who'd made that awful scene
With Boy Macfadden on the polo ground;

Both of the Granger girls, now safely married,
Isabel Pratt, whose face had grown much larger,
Still with her rather dubious Maharajah.

The Hodgsons, alas, in mourning for poor Hilda;
Vernon and Hattie Phillips from Madras,
Everyone welcoming, everyone pleased to see them,
But typically it was Ella Graves
Wearing a hideous hat and sharp with malice,
Who pounced upon them as they left the Palace.

Eleanor Graves, née Eleanor Walker,
Had always been a compulsive talker,
A fact
Which, combined with her monumental lack of tact.
Caused quite a lot of people to avoid her.
This might conceivably have annoyed her
Very much indeed
If she'd
Possessed enough humility to perceive it,
Or believe it,
But Oh no – Oh dear me no!
Her sense of superiority was so
Deeply ingrained
That she remained
Garrulous, mischievous and indiscreet,
Blandly protected by her own conceit.
'I'd no idea you were here!' she shrieked,
Inserting herself between them,
And 'It seemed like centuries,' she wailed,
Since the last time she'd seen them.
She said they *must* see her sweet new flat,
'Just pop in for drinks, or dine'
And added, with shrill irrelevance,
That Lady B's hat was divine.
They were trapped there, waiting for their car
Without a hope of escape.
The General wished she could be tied up
And gagged with adhesive tape.
It wasn't until they'd both agreed
To lunch on the following day

That at long last their car appeared
And they thankfully drove away.

It was after lunch on the next unhappy day,
When her other guests had said their 'good-byes' and
    left,
That Eleanor, insufferably mysterious,
Seized on the moment she'd been waiting for.
'There's something I just must warn you about' she
    hissed,
'And if you weren't such old and valued friends,
I wouldn't interfere or say a word,
But as I'm so fond of you and this is serious,
I thought I'd take my courage in both hands
And tell you, straight from the shoulder, what I've heard
About your Barry and that Irish character
Who, judging from all accounts, are quite inseparable.
As yet the situation's not irreparable,
But action must be taken, something done,
To salvage the reputation of your son.'

The General's eyes became cold and bleak.
He set his jaw and his face was grim.
He opened his mouth, prepared to speak,
But Lady B was too quick for him.
She rose to her feet and swiftly turned
With smiling lips and a heart of lead.
'How kind of you to be so concerned,
We're both devoted to Dan,' she said.

On leaving Eleanor's flat they took a bus
And sat in silence, worried and unhappy.
They left the bus at Prince's Gate and walked
Into the Park, still without speaking, still
Struggling to evade the implications
Of Eleanor's malign insinuations.

Sitting on two green chairs beneath the trees
They absently surveyed the London pastoral:
Nurses and children, governesses, dogs,
Two lovers sleeping in each other's arms,

A young man with his coloured shirt undone
Profiting from the unexpected sun.

Mutely they realized that here and now
It was essential for them both to face
Some of the facts of life which, hitherto,
Their inbred reticence had stowed away,
With other fixed taboos of various kinds,
Down in the depths of their sub-conscious minds.

Their self-protective innocence of course
Was not as valid as it seemed to be.
They both of them, within their private thoughts,
Knew things that neither of them would admit.
Lady B traced patterns on the ground,
With her umbrella-tip. The General frowned.

Sitting there quietly on their painted chairs
Aware that they were together, yet alone,
They watched, without noticing, the changing scene:
The brilliant sunlight of the afternoon
Softening and merging into early evening
The shadows lengthening under the London trees,
Staining with grey the brownish, trodden grass.
The summer noises seemed to be changing too
Becoming less strident as the day wore on:
The hum of traffic, buses grinding gears,
Children's shrill voices, sharp staccato barks
From those alert, exclusively London dogs
Which seem indigenous to London Parks.
Finally, stiffly, they got up and walked,
Still without speaking, back to the hotel.
In both their minds decisions had been made,
Mutually arrived at, without discussion,
And when they reached their bedroom Lady B
Took off her hat, stared in the looking-glass
And searched her face with anxious scrutiny
Discovering with relief that all the strains
And inward conflicts of the last few hours
Had left no outward traces to betray her.
Her eyes perhaps did look a trifle tired

But then, all things considered, that was not
Entirely to be wondered at. She sat
Decisively upon the bed and took
The telephone receiver from its hook.

Barry and Danny got back to the flat at six
After a rather aimless afternoon
Searching for antiques in the Brompton Road.
Barry was hot, irritable, conscious of guilt,
Because he hadn't made the slightest effort
To find out if his parents were all right
And if their glum little Kensington hotel
Was comfortable. He could have sent some flowers
If he had thought of it. He mooched about,
Took off his clothes and flung himself on the bed.
Danny looked at him quizzically and said,
'Why don't we call your rather frightening mother
And ask them both to dine somewhere or other?'

The telephone, at that moment, rang.
Barry lifted it to his ear
And suffered a further guilty pang
When his mother's voice said, 'Is that you dear?'
At any rate the evening went off well.
The Bedringtons were fetched from their hotel,
Squeezed into Danny's second-hand MG
And driven, perhaps a thought erratically,
To dine in a converted Wesleyan chapel
Called, rather whimsically, 'The Golden Apple'.

The room was tiny, lit by flickering candles.
The waiters wore canvas trousers, vests and sandals,
The menus, although very large indeed,
The General found difficult to read,
Poor Lady B in her self-conscious flurry
Rather unwisely plumped for chicken curry.

The noise was deafening, the service, slow.
Danny, resolved to make the party go,
Laid himself out, with Irish charm and wit,
To loosen up the atmosphere a bit.

And Lady B was vaguely mortified
To see the General laugh until he cried.

Later that evening, General and Lady B,
Preoccupied with their eventful day,
Slowly prepared themselves to face the night.
Lady B pensively took off her rings
And put them in the dressing-table drawer.
The General went stumping down the passage
As usual, to the bathroom, with his sponge-bag.
Lady B rubbing her face with cleansing cream,
Could hear him in the distance, gargling.
Suddenly she remembered Ella's words:
Her bland, unwarranted impertinence,
'That Irish character' 'Something must be done'
'To save the reputation of your son!'
Lady B conscious that her hands were shaking,
Made a tremendous effort at control
And, with a slight, contemptuous grimace,
Finally continued massaging her face.

On the fourth day of their dejected holiday,
Breakfasting in the hotel dining-room,
General and Lady B, without discussion,
Inspired by age-old mutual telepathy,
Arrived at the same conclusion. Lady B
Absently took some toast, then put it back.
'I think' she said, 'I'll go upstairs and pack.'

It was Danny who answered the telephone,
Barry was still asleep.
Lady B's voice was icily polite,
'I really must apologise' she said
'For calling you so early in the morning.
I'd like to have a few words with my son
However if he isn't yet awake
Please don't disturb him – You could perhaps explain,
We've had a tiresome telegram from home
Which means that we must leave immediately
And so we are leaving on the mid-day train.'
Danny, completely taken by surprise,

Tried, unsuccessfully, to sound dismayed
But Lady B cut short his protestations
Quite firmly, still implacably polite.
'Please tell him' she went on, 'that we will write
The moment we get back. It *was* such fun'
She added 'dining with you both
At that strange restaurant the other night.'

Maggie Macdonald had second sight
A loving, instinctive flair.
The telegram Lady B had sent
Confirmed her growing presentiment
That trouble was in the air.

She waited grimly to meet the train
Though her welcoming smile was gay
And while they greeted her normally
And chatted away informally
She searched their faces for signs of strain
And the signs were as clear as day.

At dinner, outwardly serene,
The General praised the salmon.
Afterwards he and Lady B
Sat for a while and watched TV
Then, gallantly loyal to routine,
Played three games of backgammon.

Maggie, knowing her mistress very well
Was certain she would not go up to bed
Without some hint, some sort of explanation
Of why they had so suddenly returned.
So, busying herself with little chores,
She put the cat out, tidied the dresser drawers,
Ironed some handkerchiefs and wound the clock,
Pottered about, arranged the breakfast tray,
Put on the kettle for a cup of tea
And finally, with nothing else to do,
She sat down in her creaking cane arm-chair
And waited for a footstep on the stair.
She heard the front door slam and knew the General

Had gone out for his customary stroll;
Silence enclosed the house, silence so deep
That the bland ticking of the kitchen clock
Sounded presumptuous, a loud intrusion,
Confusing more her heart's dismayed confusion.
Edward miaowed outside, she let him in
And, stalking before her like a conqueror,
He jumped into his basket, washed his face,
Shot her a glance and delicately yawned.
She gently massaged him behind the ears
And, unaccountably, burst into tears.

Of course, at this moment, Lady B appeared
Catching poor Maggie red-eyed and betrayed.
She paused for a moment at the door and then
Swiftly advanced and took her in her arms.
'Don't Maggie dear, please please don't cry' she said
'It isn't all that bad, really it's not.
Nothing appalling's happened, nothing sad,
Merely a tiresomeness, let's just sit down
Quite calmly and discuss it, you and me,
And, while we're at it, have a cup of tea.'

They sat there in close conference
With their crowded years behind them
Both bewildered and both distressed
But both determined to do their best
Not to allow their innocence
And prejudices to blind them.

They both knew more and they both knew less
Than either of them admitted.
To them, the infinite, complex
And strange divergencies of sex
Were based on moral capriciousness
And less to be blamed than pitied.

They both agreed that there'd always seemed
A 'difference' about Barry.
He'd never plagued them with sudden scares
Involving dubious love affairs;

Preserving himself, so they fondly dreamed,
For the girl he would finally marry.

But here they were guilty of sophistry
For, with deep, unspoken dread,
Their minds rejected the ghastly day
That would whisk their paragon away
Beyond their possessive idolatry
To an alien marriage bed.

Their earlier fears having been replaced
By faintly embarrassed relief,
They tried, with mutual urgency,
To cope with this new emergency;
Like storm-tossed mariners suddenly faced
With a strange, unchartered reef.

For more than three hours they sat there in the kitchen.
Maggie made sandwiches and brewed fresh tea.
Out in the quiet night the world was sleeping
Lulled by the murmur of the distant sea.
Finally Maggie, with shrewd common sense,
Embarked upon her speech for the defence.

'If you want my opinion' she said, 'I think
We're both of us wasting our breath.
You can't judge people by rule of thumb
And if we sit gabbling till Kingdom Come
We'll neither of us sleep a wink
And worry ourselves to death.
People are made the way they're made
And it isn't anyone's fault.
Nobody's taste can quite agree,
Some like coffee and some like tea
And Guinness rather than lemonade
And pepper rather than salt.

If Mr Barry had got caught out
By some little teenage whore
And brought her home as his blushing bride
Not only would we be mortified,

But we'd have a real problem to fuss about
And worry a great deal more.

Being a "spinster" as you might say
Not overburdened with looks,
I never went in for much romance
Though I had some fun when I got the chance
And whatever knowledge has come my way
Has come through people and books.

I don't know what this is all about
But Barry's the one I care for.
I don't mind whether he's strange or not
Or goes to bed with a Hottentot.
It's no good us trying to puzzle out
The what, the why and the wherefore.'

When Maggie's tirade came to an end
She suddenly bowed her head.
Lady B rose and kissed her cheek
And, when she could trust herself to speak
Said 'Now, my most loyal and loving friend
It's time we went up to bed.'

During the next few days the weather held.
The russet Devon cliffs cast purple shadows
Staining the edges of the quiet sea.
The General played gold, Lady B pottered
About the garden, old Mrs Macklehenny
Drove out from Saltash with her married niece,
Ate a vast luncheon and remained for tea,
On the fifth morning Lady B sat down
Purposefully at her writing-desk,
Unscrewed her fountain-pen, stared at the view,
Absently noting an old cargo ship
Lumbering across the shining bay.
The dark smoke from its funnel twisting high
Scribbled a question mark against the sky.
'My darling boy' she wrote, 'You really must
Forgive me for not writing days ago
To thank you for our little jaunt to Town.

You can't imagine how Papa and I
Enjoyed ourselves, you really were so sweet
To give your aged parents such a treat.
The weather here is perfect, not a cloud.
You'd almost think you were in Italy.
The garden's drying up of course, no rain
For nearly two whole weeks. Old Mr Drew,
The one who used to help you with your stamps,
Suddenly died last Saturday, so sad
But still, all things considered, a release,
When one is ninety-four one can't complain
At ceasing upon the midnight with no pain.
The Hilliard girls are back from Switzerland
Looking, Papa says, commoner than ever.
Hilda, the one who's said to be so clever,
Met some professor in the Engadine
And got engaged to him all in a minute!
And he's apparently quite mad and drinks
Perhaps she's not so clever as she thinks.
That's all my news and so I'd better stop
And not go rambling on like poor Aunt Jane
Who, incidentally, fell down again
Just outside Gorringe's, the poor old duck
Seems to be really haunted by bad luck.'
Lady B paused, and, nibbling her pen,
Frowned for a moment and then wrote 'P.S.
Please give our love to Danny and remember
That we expect you *both* in mid-September.'

General and Lady Bedrington
Lived on the borders of Cornwall and Devon
In a red-brick, weather-bleached Georgian house
With its distant view of the sea.
They still drove to Plymouth twice a week
In their rattling Austin Seven
And still, if the weather was feasible
Played croquet after tea.

Maggie still tramped to the village
With Black Angus, the Aberdeen.
The sun still rose and the sun still set

38

And the Eddystone light still shone.
Lady B and the General both
Encased in their daily routine
Began insensibly to forget
Their excursion to Babylon.

Personal Reminiscence

I cannot remember
I cannot remember
The house where I was born
But I know it was in Waldegrave Road
Teddington, Middlesex
Not far from the border of Surrey
An unpretentious abode
Which, I believe,
Economy forced us to leave
In rather a hurry.
But I *can* remember my grandmother's Indian shawl
Which, although exotic to behold,
Felt cold.
Then there was a framed photograph in the hall
Of my father wearing a Norfolk jacket,
Holding a bicycle and a tennis racquet
And leaning against a wall
Looking tenacious and distinctly grim
As though he feared they'd be whisked away from him.
I can also remember with repulsive clarity
Appearing at a concert in aid of charity
At which I sang, not the 'Green Hill Far Away' that you
    know
But the one by Gounod.
I remember a paper-weight made of quartz
And a sombre Gustave Doré engraving
Illustrating the 'Book of Revelations'
Which, I am told, upset my vibrations.
I remember too a most peculiar craving
For 'Liquorice All-Sorts'
Then there was a song, 'Oh that we two were Maying'

And my uncle, who later took to the bottle, playing
And playing very well
An organ called the 'Mustel'
I remember the smell of rotting leaves
In the Autumn quietness of suburban roads
And seeing the Winter river-flooding
And swirling over the tow-path by the lock.
I remember my cousin Doris in a party frock
With 'broderie anglaise' at the neck and sleeves
And being allowed to stir the Christmas pudding
On long ago, enchanted Christmas Eves.
All this took place in Teddington, Middlesex
Not far from the Surrey border
But none of these little episodes
None of the things I call to mind
None of the memories I find
Are in chronological order
Is in chronological order.

Do I believe

Do I believe in God?
Well yes, I suppose, in a sort of way.
It's really terribly hard to say.
I'm sure that there must be of course
Some kind of vital, motive force,
Some power that holds the winning cards
Behind life's ambiguous façades
But whether you think me odd or not
I can't decide if it's God or not.

I look at the changing sea and sky
And try to picture Eternity
I gaze at immensities of blue
And say to myself 'It can't be true
That somewhere up in that abstract sphere
Are all the people who once were here
Attired in white and shapeless gowns
Sitting on clouds like eiderdowns
Plucking at harps and twanging lutes
With cherubim in their birthday suits,
Set in an ageless, timeless dream
Part of a formulated scheme
Formulated before the Flood
Before the amoeba left the mud
And, stranded upon a rocky shelf
Proceeded to sub-divide itself.'

I look at the changing sea and sky
And try to picture Infinity
I gaze at a multitude of stars
Envisaging the men on Mars

Wondering if they too are torn
Between their sunset and their dawn
By dreadful, night-engendered fears
Of what may lie beyond their years
And if they too, through thick and thin,
Are dogged by consciousness of Sin.
Have they, to give them self-reliance,
A form of Martian Christian Science?
Or do they live in constant hope
Of dispensations from some Pope?

Are they pursued from womb to tomb
By hideous prophecies of doom?
Have they cathedral, church or chapel
Are they concerned with Adam's apple?
Have they immortal souls like us
Or are they less presumptuous?

Do I believe in God?
I can't say No and I can't say Yes
To me it's anybody's guess
Buf if all's true that we once were told
Before we grew wise and sad and old
When finally Death rolls up our eyes
We'll find we're in for a big surprise.

Onward Christian Soldiers

Now we have it on impeccable authority
(Without a trace of irony or mirth)
That when the Day of Judgement comes, the meek will take
    priority
And set about inheriting the earth.
In so far as I'm concerned
They can have it if they've earned
So dubious and thankless a reward
For if all that moral sanctity and snug superiority
Can seriously gratify the Lord,
Let 'em have it – let 'em keep it
Let 'em plough it – let 'em reap it
Let 'em clean it up and polish it and garnish it and sweep it.
Let 'em face up to its puzzling complexities
And, to their gentle, diffident dismay,
Discover what a crucible of hate and crime and sex it is
And start re-organising right away
But when they begin to fail
It will be of small avail
For them to turn the other silly cheek
For the Lord will smile remotely on their worries and
    perplexities
And serve them damn well right for being meek.

If I Should
Ever Wantonly Destroy

If I should ever wantonly destroy
This mechanism which is all my world
All other worlds beyond my world – all stars
All things remembered; unremembered; lost;
Imagined; dreamed of; calculated; loved;
Hated; despised; looked forward to; desired –
If I should ever wilfully escape
From what my conscience calls responsibility
From this strange, unexplained necessity
Of living life. If I should fail,
Run whimpering to death because some fear,
Because some sudden sharp neurotic dread
Some silly love, some moment of despair
Loosens me from the purpose that I hold
This sense of living life until the end
Then, only then, please pity me my friend.

Convalescence

To have been a little ill
To relax
To have Glucose and Bemax
    To be still.

To feel definitely weak
On a diet
To be ordered to be quiet,
    Not to speak.

To skim through the morning news,
To have leisure,
The ineffable, warm pleasure
    Of a snooze.

To have cooling things to drink,
Fresh Spring Flowers,
To have hours and hours and hours
    Just to think.

To have been a little ill
To have time
To invent a little rhyme
    To be still.

To have no one that you miss
    This is bliss!

I'm Here for a Short Visit Only

I'm here for a short visit only
And I'd rather be loved than hated
Eternity may be lonely
When my body's disintegrated
And that which is loosely termed my soul
Goes whizzing off through the infinite
By means of some vague, remote control
I'd like to think I was missed a bit.

Father and Son

I knew a man who believed in God
And Christian ethics and Right and Wrong,
In Life Hereafter and Angel's wings
And all the other beguiling things
That lure the tremulous soul along
From infancy to the final sod.

This pious creature believed as well
That every sparrow that fell to earth
Was duly noted by 'One Above'
In ecstasies of paternal love;
And babes that weren't baptized at birth
Were briskly fried in a tinsel hell.

He disapproved, I need hardly say,
Of carnal pleasures and bawdy jokes
And all the accoutrements of sin
(Including dancing and Gordon's gin)
And no inducement could ever coax
Him out of church on the Sabbath day.

He viewed the chaos and tears of war
As just a whim of the 'Will divine'
When youth was shattered and cities razed
He murmured smugly 'The Lord be praised'
And shot a rather annoying line
About the sins we were punished for.

He married early and took his wife,
In doleful wedlock, to Ilfracombe
Performing dutifully every rite
Appropriate to a bridal night
While no gleam pierced the pervading gloom
Of love or passion or joy of life.

He later bred, with the passing years,
Some insignificant progeny
Who genuflected and prayed and squirmed
And ultimately were all confirmed
And set in a mould of sanctity
To forge ahead with their dim careers.

But one of them (by some chance unkind;
Some strange deflection on Nature's part;
Some ancient heritage, or perhaps
Some lost, irrelevant cosmic lapse)
Showed early signs of an eager heart
And, worse than ever, a questing mind.

This unregenerate malcontent,
This septic thorn in parental flesh,
Grew up to query the Holy Writ
And, far from being ashamed of it,
Entwined his family in a mesh
Of theological argument.

He scorned the Testaments new and old,
Was unimpressed by the Holy Grail,
He scoffed at bishops and Father Knox
And every biblical paradox
He seized upon as a useful flail
To knock all mystical dogma cold.

His father shuddered, his mother cried,
His married sisters knelt down and prayed
And one stayed down for the whole of Lent
Thereby creating a precedent
Which, though not budging the renegade,
Suffused her ego with holy pride.

He grew and flourished, this Green Bay Tree,
He used his body and used his mind,
He looked on life with a cheerful eye
And when war came and he had to die
He seemed remarkably disinclined
To compromise with the Deity.

He'd lived his time and his time was done.
He'd made the most of his brief, gay years.
He'd suffered lightly his growing pains
And revelled in suns – and in winds and rains –
And loved a little and shed some tears
Without embarrassing anyone.

The funeral came, and the retinue
Of mournful relatives did their stuff.
The vicar loaded the church with prayer
And no one noticed a stranger there,
A flashy creature; a 'bit of fluff'
Who sat alone in an empty pew.

Her face was set in a stony smile.
Her hat was saucy and over smart.
She didn't weep and she didn't kneel
And though her eyes couldn't quite conceal
The misery that was in her heart,
She walked quite perkily down the aisle.

The dismal, lustreless caravan
Pursued its way to the rightful place.
The father's head was correctly bowed
But suddenly in the shuffling crowd
He saw, with horror, the brazen face
And scarlet lips of a courtesan.

His soul was seared with a burning flame;
His heart contracted with righteous wrath;
His nostrils twitched at the scent of sin
And, marching up to the Magdalene,
He barred her way on the grave-lined path
And asked her why and for what she came.

She first looked down and then raised her head.
She met his eyes and then turned aside
To where the family huddled round
That blatant hole in the sacred ground.
Her body stiffened as though with pride.
'Your son was a pal of mine' she said.

The Christian gentleman lost control
For there before him, personified,
Were aching memories, youthful tears,
The doubts and dreams that had plagued his years,
Frustrated passions and loves denied
And all the fears that had damned his soul.

He lost control and he lost his head.
His thin lips parted as though in pain
And while he quivered in every limb
It really never occurred to him
That what tormented his throbbing brain
Was bitter jealousy of the dead.

He lost control in a mist of hate,
He also forfeited Christian grace.
His chin was slavered with beads of sweat
As, with a scurrilous epithet,
He struck her brutally in the face
And thrust her roughly towards the gate.

She staggered slightly and stood at bay
Unsteadily in her high-heeled shoes.
She made a movement as though to speak,
Thought better of it and touched her cheek

Caressing gently the shameful bruise,
And then, quite quietly, walked away.

Disposing thus of the alien guest
He closed his mind to the whole affair
And, kneeling down with his kith and kin,
Soon cleansed his soul of the stink of sin.
And while he joined in subservient prayer
The son he hated was laid to rest.

I knew a man who believed in God
And Christian ethics and Right and Wrong,
But not in Nature's sublime bequest
Of fearless, passionate, human zest
That bears adventurous souls along
From infancy to the final sod.

Notes on
an Admiral's Hangover

The Admiral turned over in his dream,
His eyelids fluttered, opened, closed again.
The sky was greying on the starboard beam,
The warm air trembled with a threat of rain.
The Admiral turned over, as the pain
Battered his temples forcing him to leave
The dim-lit caverns of his sleeping brain,
And, as his outraged stomach gave a heave,
He shed a tear on his pyjama sleeve.

This then the price; the hateful reckoning;
The cold, remorseless aftermath; the truth.
How to endure this drained, bleak suffering
Bereft of the resilience of youth?
This shoddy nausea, this drab, uncouth
Submission to infernal punishment
The whip, the flail, the dreaded serpent's tooth
Were easier to bear than this descent
From what, last night, was Man omniscient.

Last night! Last night! His memory awoke
And (sharpened like some iron-barbed harpoon
Wielded by a mad fisherman, whose stroke
Stabs at the floating sickle of the moon)
Made frenzied, futile efforts to impugn
The host of images that would not stay
But swift, like coloured fish in a lagoon,
At every clumsy blundering foray,
Flirted their rainbow tails and slipped away.

The Admiral arose, and, while his hand
Tangled abstractedly his thinning hair,
Gazed through the scuttle at the hated land
No longer glamorous, no longer fair,
No more implicit with the debonair
Potential enchantments of the night,
But grey and dark, the colour of despair.
The Admiral, recoiling from the sight,
Turned to his basin and was sick outright.

Mrs Mallory

Mrs Mallory went to a Psychiatrist
On the advice of Mrs Silvera
Who had been twice divorced
And considered herself to be mal-adjusted.
Mrs Mallory, who had never been divorced at all,
Considered that she also was mal-adjusted
Not for any specific reason really
Nothing you could put your finger on
But a definite feeling of dissatisfaction
With life in general and Mr Mallory in particular,
And Deidre too who was no comfort and solace to her mother
Though at her age she should have been
But she was an unpredictable character
Who devoted too much time to 'Rock-n-Roll'
And none at all to domestic science
And helping in the house and keeping a wary eye open
For Mr Right to come along and sweep her away
To a series of social triumphs
In Washington possibly, or at least Baltimore,
Which Mrs Mallory could read about in the gossip columns
And then send the cuttings to Irma in Minneapolis
Who would have to read them whether she liked it or not.

Mrs Mallory lay on the Psychiatrist's sofa
With her arms relaxed at her sides
And her feet sticking up, one to the right and one to the left
Like a mermaid's tail.
The Psychiatrist sat behind her out of range
And waited politely for her to begin to talk
Which she was only too eager to do

After the first shyness had worn off
And he had asked her a few routine questions.
But she talked and talked and talked and talked.
So much, so much came tumbling out of her,
More than she would ever have believed possible,
But then of course, unlike Mrs Silvera, he didn't interrupt
And say things like, 'That reminds me of when I went to Atlantic
    City.
With my first husband' or 'I feel exactly the same dear naturally
But I have to control my feelings on account of being so strictly
    raised.'
The Psychiatrist didn't seem to be reminded of anything at all.
He sat there so quietly that once Mrs Mallory looked round
To see if he had dropped off, but he hadn't;
There he was scribbling away on a pad and occasionally nodding
    his head.
She told him all about Deidre
And Mr Mallory coming home from the Rotarian lunch
And taking his pants off the landing
And shouting 'Everything I have is yours, you're part of me!'
So loudly that Beulah had come out of the kitchen
And seen him with his lower parts showing
And his hat still on.
She also told the Psychiatrist about the man in the subway
Who had pressed himself against her from behind
And said something that sounded like 'Ug Ug'
Which was the one thing she had never told Mrs Silvera
Perhaps on account of her having been so strictly raised.
She told him as well about the extraordinary dream she had had
On the night following the Beedmeyer's anniversary party
But when she was in the middle of it,
Before she had even got to the bit about the horse,
He suddenly rose and smiled and said that he hoped to see her next
    Friday.
At the same time.

She got up from the couch
Feeling a little dizzy and aware that her left foot had gone to
    sleep
But when she stamped at it it was all right.
She felt much better when she got home

And much less mal-adjusted
And when Mr Mallory came home from the office
She had put on her new hostess gown
Which she had worn only twice
Once at the Beedmeyers and the other time at the Palisades
Country Club
On Christmas Eve.
Also she had rubbed some 'Shalimar' behind her ears
And greeted him with an all embracing, welcoming smile
But it was none of it any use really
When dinner was over they looked at television as they always
    did
Until it was time to go to bed,
Mr Mallory spent longer in the bathroom than usual
And the 'Shalimar' began to wear off.
But when he did come back in his pajamas
It didn't seem to matter much anyway
Because he merely belched and said 'Excuse me' automatically,
Blew her perfunctory kiss and got into his own bed,
Later on, after he had read *McCall's* for a little,
He switched off the light.

Mrs Mallory lay in the darkness
With her arms relaxed at her sides
And her feet up, one to the right and one to the left
Like a mermaid's tail
And a tear rolled down her face all the way to her chin.

DEATH

"The thrill has gone,
To linger on
Would spoil it anyhow,
Let's creep away from the day
For the Party's over now."

Words and Music

When I Have Fears

When I have fears, as Keats had fears,
Of the moment I'll cease to be
I console myself with vanished years
Remember laughter, remembered tears,
And the peace of the changing sea.

When I feel sad, as Keats felt sad,
That my life is so nearly done
It gives me comfort to dwell upon
Remembered friends who are dead and gone
And the jokes we had and the fun.

How happy they are I cannot know
But happy am I who loved them so.

1901

When Queen Victoria died
The whole of England mourned
Not for a so recently breathing old woman
A wife and a mother and a widow,
Not for a staunch upholder of Christendom,
A stickler for etiquette
A vigilant of moral values
But for a symbol.
A symbol of security and prosperity
Of 'My Country Right or Wrong'
Of 'God is good and Bad is bad'
And 'What was good enough for your father
Ought to be good enough for you'
And 'If you don't eat your tapioca pudding
You will be locked in your bedroom
And given nothing but bread and water
Over and over again until you come to your senses
And are weak and pale and famished and say
Breathlessly, hopelessly and with hate in your heart
"Please Papa I would now like some tapioca pudding very much
    indeed"'
A symbol too of proper elegance
Not the flaunting, bejewelled kind
That became so popular
But a truly proper elegance,
An elegance of the spirit,
Of withdrawal from unpleasant subjects
Such as Sex and Poverty and Pit Ponies
And Little Children working in the Mines
And Rude Words and Divorce and Socialism
And numberless other inadmissible horrors.

When Queen Victoria died
They brought her little body from the Isle of Wight
Closed up in a black coffin, finished and done for,
With no longer any feelings and regrets and Memories of Albert
And no more blood pumping through the feeble veins
And no more heart beating away
As it had beaten for so many tiring years.
The coffin was placed upon a gun-carriage
And drawn along sadly and slowly by English sailors.

But long before this the people had mourned
And walked about the streets and the Parks and Kensington
    Gardens
Silently, solemnly and dressed in black.
Now, with the news already a few days old
The immediate shock had faded.
The business of the funeral was less poignant than the first realization
    of death,
This was a pageant, right and fitting, but adjustments were already
    beginning to be made.
This was something we were all used to,
This slow solemnity
This measured progress to the grave.
If it hadn't been for the gun-carriage
And the crowds and all the flags at half mast
And all the shops being closed
It might just as well have been Aunt Cordelia
Who died a few months earlier in Torquay
And had to be brought up to London by the Great Western
In a rather large coffin
And driven slowly, oh so slowly
To the family burial ground at Esher
With all the relatives driving behind
Wearing black black black and peering furtively out of the carriage
    windows
To note for a moment that life was going on as usual.
For Aunt Cordelia was no symbol really
And her small death was of little account.
She was, after all, very old indeed
Although not quite so old as Queen Victoria
But on the other hand she didn't have so much prestige

Except of course in her own personal mind
And that was snuffed out at the same moment as everything else
Also, unlike Queen Victoria, she had few mourners
Just the family and Mrs Stokes who had been fond of her
And Miss Esme Banks who had looked after her in Torquay
And two remote cousins
Who couldn't rightly be classed as family
Because they were so very far removed
And only came to the cemetary because it was a sign of respect,
Respect, what is more, without hope
For there was little or no likelihood of their being mentioned in
    the will
But there they were all the same
Both tall and bent, in black toques with veils,
And both crying.

When Queen Victoria died
And was buried and the gun-carriage was dragged empty away
    again
The shops reopened and so did the theatres
Although business was none too good.
But still it improved after a while
And everyone began to make plans for the Coronation
And it looked as if nothing much had happened
And perhaps nothing much had really
Except that an era, an epoch, an attitude of mind, was ended.

There would be other eras and epochs and attitudes of mind.
But never quite the same.

Condolence

The mind, an inveterate traveller
Journeys swiftly and far
Faster than light, quicker than sound
Or the flaming arc of a falling star
But the body remains in a vacuum
Gagged, bound and sick with dread
Knowing the words that can't be spoken
Searching for words that must be said
Dumb, inarticulate, heartbroken.
Inadequate, inhibited.

Nothing is Lost

Deep in our sub-conscious, we are told
Lie all our memories, lie all the notes
Of all the music we have ever heard
And all the phrases those we loved have spoken,
Sorrows and losses time has since consoled,
Family jokes, out-moded anecdotes
Each sentimental souvenir and token
Everything seen, experienced, each word
Addressed to us in infancy, before
Before we could even know or understand
The implications of our wonderland.
There they all are, the legendary lies
The birthday treats, the sights, the sounds, the tears
Forgotten debris of forgotten years
Waiting to be recalled, waiting to rise
Before our world dissolves before our eyes
Waiting for some small, intimate reminder,
A word, a tune, a known familiar scent
An echo from the past when, innocent
We looked upon the present with delight
And doubted not the future would be kinder
And never knew the loneliness of night.

The Great Awakening

As I awoke this morning
When all sweet things are born
A robin perched upon my sill
To signal the coming dawn.
The bird was fragile, young and gay
And sweetly did it sing
The thoughts of happiness and joy
Into my heart did bring.
I smiled softly at the cheery song
Then as it paused, a moment's lull,
I gently closed the window
And crushed its fucking skull.

FRIENDS . . . AND OTHERS

Friends

"Ever since that first day we met
We both of us guessed
Many a sun would rise and set
Before we coalesced"

Together with Music

Any Part of Piggy

Any part of piggy
Is quite all right with me
Ham from Westphalia, ham from Parma
Ham as lean as the Dalai Lama
Ham from Virginia, ham from York,
Trotters, sausages, hot roast pork.
Crackling crisp for my teeth to grind on
Bacon with or without the rind on
Though humanitarian
I'm not a vegetarian.
I'm neither crank nor prude nor prig
And though it may sound infra dig
Any part of darling pig.
Is perfectly fine with me.

To Meg Titheradge*

This lyric tribute is addressed to Meg's
Enthusiastic, hardy little legs
And also, as we're handing out awards,
To her supremely vocal vocal-chords.
How strange that so minute a throat could nurture
A larynx clearly made of gutta-percha.
And how more strange (and jolly nice of course)
That so much harnessed locomotive force
Should be condensed in so 'petite' a creature
Whose charm is not her least distinctive feature.
And so this band; this company; this group;
This happy breed of vagabonds; this troupe;
This Noël Coward galaxy; this Rep;
Await with pleasure your unfailing step
And fondly hope, when Judgement day befall us
That you dear Meg will not omit to call us.

* Meg Titheradge was a member of the Company which toured with Noël during
the War in *Present Laughter, Blithe Spirit* and *This Happy Breed.*

To Mary MacArthur*

With pleasure Miss MacArthur dear
I venture to inscribe
The following polite, sincere
And gentle diatribe.

To one fact pray be reconciled
Admit no 'ifs' nor 'buts'
Your mother is an Actress, child
And consequently, 'Nuts'.

There's one more fact that you must list
And face for good or bad.
Your father is a Dramatist
And obviously mad.

Whichever way your fortune bends
And circumstances change
Your mother's and your father's friends
Are certain to be strange.

In all this odd eccentric clan
Just one exception shines
The *talented* and *witty* man
Who wrote these *charming* lines!

*Mary MacArthur was born in 1933, the daughter of the actress Helen Hayes and
playwright Charles MacArthur.

Reply – Reply

Dear General, Dear Mason-Mac*
Dear Excellence, Sir Noël
How terrible that I've come back
Too late to save your soel!

I'm lacerated to the quick
Knowing the verse you greet me with
Merely provides a moral stick
For your loved ones to beat me with.

How can I happily appear
Before your wife and daughter
Knowing that you, whom they revere,
Have been on such a 'snorter'?

Knowing how freely you imbibe
Without the least contrition
How can I honestly describe
The triumph of your mission?

How can I praise your skill and tact
In dealing with Badoglio
Faced with the miserable fact
Of this obscene imbroglio?

Why have you placed the blame on me
For this wild, alcoholic,
Most shaming and most utterly
Abominable frolic?

When, on the flimsiest excuse
You grab the nearest bottle
What in the world is any use
What'll I tell them, what'll? - - - !

*Noel worked during the War with Lt.-Gen. Sir (Frank) Noël Mason-Macfarlane
(1889-1953), who at the time was Director of Military Intelligence with the British
Expeditionary Force.

Goldeneye Calypso*

Mongoose dig about sunken garden
Mongoose murmur 'Oh my – Oh my!
No more frig about – beg your pardon
Things are changing at Goldeneye!'

Mongoose say to Annee
Mongoose say to Annee
Your man shady as mango tree
Sweet as honey from bee.

Hey for the Alka-Seltzer
Ho for the Aspirin
Hey for the saltfish, ackee, ganja, Booby's eggs, Gordon's gin.

Mongoose listen to white folks wailin'
Mongoose giggle, say, 'Me no deaf.
No more waffle and Daily Mailin'
Annie Rothermere's Madam F.'

Mongoose say to Annee
Carlyle Mansions N.G.
Goldeneye a catastrophee
Whitecliffs too near the sea.

Hey for the blowfish, blowfish.
Ho for the wedding ring
Hey for the Dry Martinis, old goat fricassee, Old Man's Thing.

Mongoose love human sacrifices
Mongoose snigger at Human Race
Can't have wedding without the Bryces,
Both the Stephensons, Margaret Case.

Mongoose say to Annee
Now you get your decree
Once you lady of high degree
Now you common as me.

Hey for the piggly-wigly
Ho for the wedding dress
Hey for the Earl of Dudley, Loelia Westminster, Kemsley
    Press.

*Goldeneye was the name of the house in Jamaica where writer Ian Fleming lived with
Ann Rothermere (later Mrs Fleming of the newspaper family). After staying there,
Noël renamed the house 'Goldeneye, Nose, Throat and Ear'.

Goldeneye Opus No 2

Ah, Goldeneye! Sedate, historic pile
Haven of peace for those in dire distress
Welcome oasis in a wilderness
Of dreadful rumour and most wild surmise
Dear sanctuary, screened from prying eyes
Sylvan retreat, impregnable and kind
Giver of solace to the weary mind
To you, to you we fly to rest awhile
Here to this gracious home, this grateful harbour
Wrought, not by Vanburgh, but Scovell and Barber.

Here, in this paradise of palm and pine
(Perhaps not pine but anyhow sea-grape)
The hunted and the harassed may escape
The troubled and tormented may relax
And lie about at ease in shorts and slacks
Wincing a bit perhaps when sunlight falls
On all those horse's arses around the walls
But soothed by architectural design
Wishing the wicked world could be as well built
As this old shack that Barber and Scovell built.

To L. R-M*

There are certain ladies in our land,
Still living and still unafraid
Whose hearts have known a lot of pain,
Whose eyes have shed so many tears,
Who welcomed pity with disdain
And view the fast encroaching years
Humorously and undismayed.

There are certain ladies in our land,
Whose courage is too deeply bred
To merit unreflecting praise.
For them no easy, glib escape;
No mystic hopes confuse their days
They can identify the shape
Of what's to come, devoid of dread.

There are certain ladies in our land
Who bring to Life the gift of gay
Uncompromising sanity.
The past, for them, is safe and sure
Perhaps their only vanity
Is that they know they can endure
The rigours of another day.

*Linda Rhodes-Moorhouse was one of Noël's circle of friends during the 1950s.

'Morning Glory'
Epic in Commemoration of the 50th Anniversary of the *Daily Mail*

All Harmsworths, Northcliffes, Rothermeres
Deserve from us resounding cheers
While Camroses and Beaverbrooks
Have earned from us the blackest looks
And Kemsley to his lasting spleen
Is nothing but a might-have-been
And all because through hail and snow
The *Daily Mail* has charmed us so
In Peace and War and flood and fight
The *Daily Mail* is *always* right
Through famine, pestilence and strike
The *Daily Mail* says what *we* like
To Tory truths and Labour lies
This *lovely* paper puts us wise
Although our bloody heads are bowed
This *darling* paper does us proud
In any crisis that occurs
This *angel* paper *never* errs
This classic home of journalese
Where ne'er a cliché fails to please
This epic of the printing press
We humbly and devoutly bless.
O amiable, devoted, kind,
Impeccable, serene, refined
Most exquisite, most dignified,
Dear emblem of our Nation's pride.

In case some feeble mind should miss
The point of this analysis
I wrote it at the firm and clear
Request of Lady Rothermere.

Tribute to Marlene Dietrich*

We know God made trees
And the birds and the bees
And the seas for the fishes to swim in
We are also aware
That he has quite a flair
For creating exceptional women.
When Eve said to Adam
'Start calling me Madam'
The world became far more exciting
Which turns to confusion
The modern delusion
That sex is a question of lighting
For female allure
Whether pure or impure
Has seldom reported a failure
As I know and you know
From Venus and Juno
Right down to La Dame aux Camélias.
This glamour, it seems,
Is the substance of dreams
To the most imperceptive perceiver
The Serpent of Nile
Could achieve with a smile
Far quicker results than Geneva.
Though we all might enjoy
Seeing Helen of Troy
As a gay, cabaret entertainer

I doubt that she could
Be one quarter as good
As our legendary, lovely Marlene.

*Noël wrote this as his own introduction for the International star Marlene Dietrich
when she appeared in cabaret in London at the Café de Paris in 1954.

Sonnet to a Hermit Crab

These lines are written to a Hermit Crab.
O singular amphibian recluse!
Your predatoriness has this excuse,
That Nature fashioned you to smash and grab;
To be content with neither stone nor slab
But to appropriate for your own use
The homes of others. What perverse, obtuse,
Unkindly God designed a life so drab?
You have strong forward claws; a heart of steel,
But when your stolen shell becomes too tight
Out you must go, a larger one to find.
How sad to think that your Achilles heel
Lies in your mortifying, brownish-white,
Too vulnerable and too soft behind!

OTHERS

"There are bad times just around the corner,
There are dark clouds hurtling through the sky
And it's no use whining
About a silver lining
For we *know* from experience that they won't roll by"

The Globe Revue

Open Letter to a Mayor

Dear Mr. Mayor, I feel myself impelled
By some strong impulse that will not be quelled
To ask you, just for once, to put aside
Your urban dignity, your civic pride
And answer me a question fair and square.
Now, man to man, or rather man to Mayor:
What evil circumstances; what obscene desire;
What aberration; what witches' fire;
What hidden complex in your early life
Caused you to choose quite such a horrid wife?
Were you ensnared? If so, with what? and how?
To what bleak magic did your spirit bow?
How could she, even in her younger years,
Ever have *not* bored everyone to tears?
How, e'en when dandled on her mother's arm,
Could she have shown the slightest sign of charm?
Could I but see in this her present mould
Some remnant of a beauty since grown old,
Could I imagine, in some vanished Spring,
This squat, unlissom figure gambolling,
Could I, for just one instant, find a trace
Of erstwhile kindness in that metal face
Then Mr. Mayor, I would have held my peace,
But as it is I find I cannot cease
To ponder, wonder, query, question why?
(Considering the adequate supply
Of women amiable, of women kind,
Of women clever, flexible of mind,
Of women glamorous, of women smart,
Of women sensuous and warm of heart)
Why why why why dear Mayor did you select

A woman so determined to reject
All canons of politeness, every grace.
A woman so determined to efface
From social life all pleasantness and tact
A woman so unfitted to enact
A role quite obviously not designed
To suit a paltry soul, a meagre mind?
A role in fact of graciousness and charm,
Of kindliness to strangers and of calm,
Untroubled manners. Mr. Mayor, I hate
So unequivocally to have to state
That she to whom you gave your honoured name,
With whom you proudly from the Altar came
With whom you cheerfully agreed to share
The arduous travail of being Mayor,
This creature whose exaggerated sense
Of her importance, whose grotesque, immense
Conviction that she's witty, worldly wise,
Unfailingly attractive in men's eyes,
Outspoken, frank, unmatched in repartee,
Bewilders me. What can the basis be
For these delusions? Is she stricken blind
Before her mirror? Has God been too kind
And cunningly contrived her inner ear
So that each time she speaks she cannot hear
The cliché and the antiquated quips
That fall with such assurance from her lips?
Oh! Mr. Mayor, forgive me if you can
Reply to me quite frankly, Mayor to man.
Why did you marry her, what bitter fate
Led you towards so sinister a mate?
What siren's call, what shrill malignant voice
Lured you to such a miserable choice?
What devil's angel with dank wings outspread
Persuaded you to share your civic bed
With such a dull, unprepossessing, rude,
Unequalled Queen of social turpitude?
Why did you do it and thus let her loose

Upon the city? What was your excuse?
Answer me please, pray set my mind at ease
What did you do it for? please tell me – please.

With curiosity my mind's devoured
I am, yours most sincerely, Noël Coward.

Lines to a Little God

There's just one little God I'd like to meet,
Not a Big-Shot, not the All Highest Head Boy.
I've quite a few complaints with which to greet
My Judges on the day that I'm a dead boy.
The God that I particularly itch
To say just one vituperative word to,
Is that sardonic, mean son of a bitch
Whom no religious sect has yet referred to,
That under-God whose whole-time job it is
To organise our minor miseries.

Not our great sorrows; not the bitter pain
Of anguished last good-byes; not death; nor blindness;
Nor yet the agonising mental strain
Imposed on us by pious loving-kindness.
Not melancholia; not sex-frustration;
Not hope abandoned; not the toll of war;
Nor the unutterable desolation
Of an illusion dead for evermore.
But each and every little sting that serves
To agitate and lacerate our nerves.

That little pig; that sly, sadistic Goebbels
Who makes the windows rattle in the night,
Who shrewdly times the intermittent burbles
Of water pipes when I am trying to write.

Who so arranges that my next door neighbours
Elect to have some friends in for a drink
When, wearied by my histrionic labours,
I snatch an hour in bed to rest and think.
Who also, at five-thirty in the morning,
Sets off an accidental air-raid warning.

This beastly little God, this misbegotten
Smart-Alec whose whole livelihood depends
On fixing that the one song I've forgotten
Should be demanded loudly by my friends.
Who also plans for hotel maids to call me
Briskly with cups of tea at half-past seven.
Whatever dire punishments befall me
When I meet this rat at the bar of Heaven
I'll rip his star-spun, butter muslin frock off
And knock his sneering, bloody little block off.

The Ballad of Graham Greene*

Oh there's many a heart beats faster, lads,
And swords from their sheathes flash keen
When round the embers – the glowing embers
Men crouch at Hallowe'en.
And suddenly somebody remembers
The name of Graham Greene!
(A literary disaster lads
The fall of Graham Greene.)

Oh there's many a Catholic Priest, my boys,
And many a Rural Dean
Who, ages later – long ages later
When all has been, has been,
Will secretly read an old *Spectator*
And pray for Graham Greene.
(Let's hope its sales have decreased my boys
Because of Graham Greene.)

Oh one asks oneself and one's God, my lads,
Was ever a mind so mean,
That could have vented – so shrilly vented
Such quantities of spleen
Upon a colleague? Unprecedented!
Poor Mr. Graham Greene.
(One's pride forbids one to nod, my lads,
To Mr. Graham Greene.)

Oh there's many a bitter smile my boys
And many a sneer obscene
When any critic – a first-rate critic,
Becomes a 'Might have been'

Through being as harsh and Jesuitic
As Mr. Graham Greene.
(Restrain that cynical smile, my boys,
To jeer is never worth while, my boys.
Remember the rising bile, my boys,
Of Mr. Graham Greene.)

*'Perhaps it is unnecessary to state that the above was written in June 1941 fol-
lowing two very unpleasant attacks on me and my work by Mr Graham Greene
in the *Spectator*.' N.C.

In giving his approval for the inclusion of this verse in the current collection,
Graham Greene said 'He (Noël) had every reason to be angry with me at that
moment, although we became friends later.'

In Masculine Homage

She was as pretty as she could be,
A terribly charming lady.
She wore her hat like a bridal wreath,
And flashed her small American teeth;
Demanding of men an awed submission,
Polite obeisance to her Tradition.
Which was, for those who had eyes to see,
The age old feminine fallacy
That women live strange, mysterious lives,
With intuitions as sharp as knives.
With streaks of innocence, pure as snow,
And small, sly secrets, men mustn't know.
Her neck was white, and her hands were slim,
And she had a son, and seemed fond of him.
He was ten, or twelve, so of course she'd been
A married woman at seventeen.
She used her eyes to arouse a man,
But she lacked the warmth of a Courtesan.
She was as pretty as she could be,
A tediously charming lady.

Political Hostess

The Lady Alexandra Innes-Hooke,
Apart from her inherent social grace,
Knew everyone, seldom forgot a face,
Read everything, not just the latest book
And, in her charming house in Seymour Place,
Was shrewd enough to have a perfect cook.

Her luncheons and her dinner parties were
Attended by a 'chic' and motley crew.
There the Gentile rubbed shoulders with the Jew;
Belgravia hobnobbed with Bloomsbury Square,
Writers and Painters, Actors too were there,
Statesmen and Politicians and a few
Foreigners (Herr Professor – Cher Confrère).

Politically speaking, Lady A
Was, shall we say, a trifle volatile?
She listened, without prejudice or guile
To what her guests, too freely, had to say
On the immediate problems of the day
Then, with a knowing, enigmatic smile.
Misquoted them when they had gone away.

Thus, in those years when all our pride had fled,
When all our policies were misconceived,
The Lady Alexandra soon achieved
A reputation as a fountain-head
Of inside information. What she said
Was widely, and too frequently believed.
(Many of those believers are now dead).

A long way back, in nineteen twenty-nine,
She hinted darkly that we had misused
The German Nation. Loudly she accused
Both French and British statesmen of malign,
Ungenerous behaviour to a fine
And cultured Race. She later on refused
To comment, when they occupied the Rhine.

During the 'idiotic' Spanish war
Non-Intervention seemed to her to be
Not only right and sensible, but *the*
Only solution. No one could be more
Unprejudiced or democratic nor
Unmindful of the changing world than she,
But 'Reds' were dangerous and worse, a bore.

During the Abyssinian campaign
She was vociferous and rather shrill.
'Why' she exclaimed, 'Should we impose our will
On Mussolini? Why should we maintain
This silly "governess" attitude again?
How could he be expected to fulfil
His obligations without more Terrain?'

During the Abdication she was dim.
Only when pressed she'd wistfully aver
That tho' she never really cared for 'her'
She'd always been extremely fond of 'him'.
The coming coronation would be grim,
She said, a revolution might occur.
'Alors, tant pis, il faut baisser or swim!'

In nineteen thirty-eight she reached her peak
Of bathos. The intolerable strain
Of that degrading year addled her brain
To such a sad extent that she would shriek
At anyone who'd even an oblique
Distrust of Mr. Neville Chamberlain.
(This view unhappily was not unique.)

In March when Hitler 'ratified' his pact
By walking into Prague, her mind was clear.
'It really couldn't matter less my dear'
She said, 'The tiresome little man attacked
Because he couldn't very well retract'.
She added: 'There will be no war this year.
This is not wishful thinking, it's a fact'.

From nineteen thirty-nine to 'forty-two
The Lady Alexandra poured out tea
In various canteens from two 'til three.
Later, an influential man she knew,
(One of the many, *not* one of the Few)
Arranged for her to join the B.B.C.
(Only as an adviser, it is true).

A little later still she thought she'd try
To see if she could broadcast on her own.
Altho' she'd never seen a microphone
They let her do three Postscripts in July.
And when some beast in Parliament asked why
In an exceedingly sarcastic tone,
Her friend transferred her to the M. of I.

Thus Lady Alexandra Innes-Hooke,
Altho' her house in Seymour Place has gone,
Still bravely serves Perfidious Albion
And, like Lord Tennyson's annoying brook,
Goes on and on and on and on and on.

To Mr. James Agate*

Mr. James Agate
Arrived late.
As a matter of fact
He missed half the first Act.
Then, in the Circle Bar,
Whence Bacchus beckoned,
He missed most of the Second,
Discussing Milton's blindness,
Thus going too far,
From which I reckoned
That he would skip the Third.
But I was wrong, far worse occurred,
He fell asleep!
There in his seat on the aisle
He dozed awhile.
Authors may weep
At such unkindness
But other than author's tears;
The ghosts of earlier years.
His own shades, his proprietary ghosts
Whom he reveres;
All those of whom he boasts
Of having seen, remembered; these would cry
More bitterly, more sorrowfully than I.
His Sarah, his Réjane and his Rachel,
(He can't remember her but he can tell
Many an anecdote
About her, and can quote
From *Phèdre*
Alas, he never quotes from *Cavalcèdre!*)

How these would sob
To see so 'vrai' a critic,
So 'blasé' a critic,
So 'gonflé' a critic
Let down his job!

*James Agate was the distinguished drama critic of the *Sunday Times*.

Quiet Old Timers

I love to think of Mr. Stamps
Whose supercilious prattle
Which, like a strange celestial croup
Inspired by The Oxford Group,
Can spread the Word of God to tramps
Who wish to reach Seattle.

I love to think of Mrs. Stamps
At one time faintly flighty
Who, changing from a draggled dove
Into a paragon of love,
In these days only really vamps
Her boy friend The Almighty.

I love to think of both the Stamps
In conjugal seclusion
Tightly encased in thought sublime
Having a dreadfully quiet time
Bearing with pride the mental cramps
Of mystical illusion.

The Lady at the Party

Look at her sitting there
A little way apart; her tortured hair
Twisted and bullied into brittle curls
Ape-ing the more flamboyant 'Glamour Girls'

Notice her beady eyes
In action, as her sordid trade she plies.
Watch her lean forward smiling, strained to hear
Some note of discord in the atmosphere,

Some little private sigh
Uttered unconsciously in passing by,
A 'nuance' normal ears might well have missed
But not those of a lady columnist.

What was the circumstance?
What freak of destiny, what horrid chance,
What disillusionment, what venom'd spur
Goaded this wretched human scavenger

Drearily to decide
To jettison all decency and pride
And choose a life whose livelihood depends
Upon the private sorrows of her friends?

See how polite they are!
Bringing her this and that, going too far,
Showing too clearly in their votive flights
How much they fear the column that she writes.

Where does the answer lie?
Is the demand creating the supply
Enough excuse for pandering to dead,
Decaying minds, to earn your daily bread?

What is it worth in gold?
This sale of human dignity, this cold,
Ignoble, calculating, drab descent
Into the drains of social excrement?

When, in the future years
(Beyond publicity, beyond the tears
Her cheerful, base betrayals caused to flow)
She's near to death, will she that instant know

How much despair and pain
Was wrought by her salacious, vulgar brain?
Or will she, in the shadow of the hearse,
Suspect the priest of flirting with the nurse?

Pity her if you can
This haunted, mediocre harridan
Haunted by fear; a puzzled sense of loss,
And all the lives she's nailed upon the cross.

From One Chap to Another
A Complaint

I told the Desboroughs about my wife
And they couldn't have minded less,
I also told them about my life
In the heart of the F.M.S.*

I also told them she had red hair
But the snooty Desboroughs didn't care;
I mentioned once that we had a child
And the beastly Desboroughs merely smiled.
I chanced to mention the Sultan's Aunt
Who had given my wife a rubber plant,
I also mentioned, in passing, twice
That the Chinese merchants were awfully nice
And so adored me, the simple souls
That they gave me presents of several scrolls
With my name at the top in a Chinese hand
Which none but the Chinese understand.
I also showed them a queen Sarong
A gift from the Sultan of Lang Kwi Kiong
And a slightly rusty Malayan knife
Which was forced on me by the Sultan's wife.
When I tried to describe a Malay dawn
The odious Desboroughs suppressed a yawn.
When I showed them the Rajah's private sword
The haughty Desboroughs were frankly bored
So discerning between us no clear bond
I dine each night with a cendré blonde
From whom it is easy to invoke
A winsome laugh at the oldest joke

And she sits quite still in a low cut dress
And is frightfully thrilled with the F.M.S.

I told the Desboroughs about my wife
And they couldn't have looked more dead,
I also told them about my life
And they giggled and went to bed.

*F.M.S.: Federated Malay States.

Let These People Go

I wish the intellectuals,
The clever ones,
Would go to Russia.
Those who have University Degrees,
Those 'Leftist' boys and girls
Who argue so well
About the 'Workers' Rights'
And 'Man's True Destiny' and the delights
Of equal independence, State controlled.
Let them leave England please
If our traditions hold
No magic for them; if new Gods compel
Their very new allegiance, let them go.
Those ardent ineffectuals
Were never ones
To do much more than analyse,
Very meticulously, our defects
Of Government and Empire. They're too wise
To care about our Past: 'England Expects
Each man to do his duty'. Theirs is clear,
To go to Russia.
Why should they linger here?
Where they can hardly flush a
Toilet without explaining carefully why,
And how, such bourgeois actions signify
Capitalistic greed and retrogression
And oppression.
Their place is overseas.
Not where the British Raj
The hated flag unfurls;
Perish such thoughts!

Not where the natives cringe,
Bullied and crushed wherever British rule is
And where the bloated Englishman, half drunk, in shorts,
Forces the gentle, uncomplaining coolies
To do all sorts
Of most degrading things, including Sports.
No. No. Russia is large.
England is very small
And we have little space
For those who only can perceive disgrace
In our achievements. As they seem to know
So very clearly
That our Empire's tottering on the fringe
Of final dissolution
(Rightly of course,
A just and fitting punishment for all
Our unregenerate displays of force,
We must pay dearly
For those uncouth, dishonourable deeds.
Long live the Revolution!
Our Grenvilles, Raleighs, Drakes,
Our Good Queen Besses,
Our braggart Marlboroughs, Wellingtons and Clives
Were those who brought us low,
And though
The shameful memory of them still survives,
The Soul of Man, the Human Spirit, bleeds
At their excesses.
God! Let these people go.
Not for their own so much as for our sakes.
We don't require them,
Nor can we much admire them
Measured against our much less enlightened,
Unflurried and unfrightened
True citizens. Far better they should be
Proving their theories amidst alien snow
Where men are free
And equal with each other. Let them trot
Off to that other earth, that other plot,
That demi-Paradise, that teeming womb
Of other values. There till the crack of Doom

Let them remain
And multiply contentedly. And when in
The years to come, if they should entertain
A doubt or two,
All that they have to do
To reassure themselves and find again
Their lost illusions, is to join the queue
Standing in snow before that foreign tomb,
And reverently have a look at Lenin.

What a Saucy Girl.

Steady, steady, Mary Baker Eddy*
You've got to play the final scene
Admit that it's distasteful
To say that pain ain't painful –
But what about some more morphine?
In your great flight with sin, come
Admit you made an income
Far greater than your friend the Nazarene.
Steady, steady, Mary Baker Eddy
What a saucy girl you've been!

*Discoverer and founder of Christian Science. Lived 1821-1910.

THEATRICAL . . .
AND MUSICAL

THEATRICAL

"Don't put your daughter on the stage, Mrs Worthington
Don't put your daughter on the stage,
The profession is overcrowded
And the struggle's pretty tough."

Mrs Worthington

The Boy Actor

I can remember. I can remember.
The months of November and December
  Were filled for me with peculiar joys
So different from those of other boys
  For other boys would be counting the days
Until end of term and holiday times
  But I was acting in Christmas plays
While they were taken to pantomimes.
  I didn't envy their Eton suits,
Their children's dances and Christmas trees.
  My life had wonderful substitutes
For such conventional treats as these.
  I didn't envy their country larks,
Their organized games in panelled halls:
  While they made snow-men in stately parks
I was counting the curtain calls.

  I remember the auditions, the nerve-racking auditions:
  Darkened auditorium and empty, dusty stage,
  Little girls in ballet dresses practising 'positions'
  Gentlemen with pince-nez asking you your age.
  Hopefulness and nervousness struggling within you,
  Dreading that familiar phrase, 'Thank you dear, no more.'
  Straining every muscle, every tendon, every sinew
  To do your dance much better than you'd ever done
      before.
  Think of your performance. Never mind the others,
  Never mind the pianist, talent must prevail.
  Never mind the baleful eyes of other children's mothers
  Glaring from the corners and willing you to fail.

I can remember. I can remember.
The months of November and December
    Were more significant to me
Than other months could ever be
    For they were the months of high romance
When destiny waited on tip-toe,
    When every boy actor stood a chance
Of getting into a Christmas show,
    Not for me the dubious heaven
Of being some prefect's protégé!
    Not for me the Second Eleven.
For me, two performances a day.

        Ah those first rehearsals! Only very few lines:
        Rushing home to mother, learning them by heart,
        'Enter Left through window' – Dots to mark the cue lines:
        'Exit with the others' – Still it *was* a part.
        Opening performance; legs a bit unsteady,
        Dedicated tension, shivers down my spine,
        Powder, grease and eye-black, sticks of make-up ready
        Leichner number three and number five and number nine.
        World of strange enchantment, magic for a small boy
        Dreaming of the future, reaching for the crown,
        Rigid in the dressing-room, listening for the call-boy
        'Overture Beginners – Everybody Down!'

I can remember. I can remember.
The months of November and December,
    Although climatically cold and damp,
Meant more to me than Aladdin's lamp.
I see myself, having got a job,
Walking on wings along the Strand,
Uncertain whether to laugh or sob
And clutching tightly my mother's hand,
    I never cared who scored the goal
Or which side won the silver cup,
    I never learned to bat or bowl
But I heard the curtain going up.

Epitaph for
an Elderly Actress

She got in a rage
About age
And retired, in a huff, from the stage.
Which, taken all round, was a pity
Because she was still fairly pretty
But she got in a rage
About age.

She burst into tears
It appears
When the rude, inconsiderate years
Undermined her once flawless complexion
And whenever she saw her reflection
In a mirror, she burst into tears
It appears.

She got in a state
About weight
And resented each morsel she ate.
Her colon she constantly sluiced
And reduced and reduced and reduced
And, at quite an incredible rate
Put on weight.

She got in a rage
About age
But she still could have played Mistress Page
And she certainly could have done worse
Than *Hay Fever* or Juliet's Nurse
But she got in a terrible rage
About age.

And she moaned and she wept and she wailed
And she roared and she ranted and railed
And retired, very heavily, veiled,
From the stage.

Social Grace

I expect you've heard this a million times before
But I absolutely adored your last play
I went four times – and now to think
That here I am actually talking you!
It's thrilling! Honestly it is, I mean,
It's always thrilling isn't it to meet someone really celebrated?
I mean someone who really does things.
I expect all this is a terrible bore for you.
After all you go everywhere and know everybody.
It must be wonderful to go absolutely everywhere
And know absolutely everybody and – Oh dear –
Then to have to listen to someone like me,
I mean someone absolutely ordinary just one of your public.
No one will believe me when I tell them
That I have actually been talking to the great man himself.
It must be wonderful to be so frightfully brainy
And know all the things that you know
I'm not brainy a bit, neither is my husband,
Just plain humdrum, that's what we are.
But we do come up to town occasionally
And go to shows and things. Actually my husband
Is quite a critic, not professionally of course,
What I mean is that he isn't all that easily pleased.
He doesn't like everything. Oh no not by any means.
He simply hated that thing at the Haymarket
Which everybody went on about. 'Rubbish' he said,
Straight out like that, 'Damned Rubbish!'
I nearly died because heaps of people were listening.
But that's quite typical of him. He just says what he thinks.

And he can't stand all this highbrow stuff –
Do you know what I mean? – All these plays about people being
   miserable
And never getting what they want and not even committing
   suicide
But just being absolutely wretched. He says he goes to the
   theatre
To have a good time. That's why he simply loves all your things,
I mean they relax him and he doesn't have to think.
And he certainly does love a good laugh.
You should have seen him the other night when we went to that
   film
With what's-her-name in it – I can't remember the title.
I thought he'd have a fit, honestly I did.
You must know the one I mean, the one about the man who comes
   home
And finds his wife has been carrying on with his best friend
And of course he's furious at first and then he decides to teach her
   a lesson.
You must have seen it. I wish I could remember the name
But that's absolutely typical of me, I've got a head like a sieve,
I keep on forgetting things and as for names – well!
I just cannot for the life of me remember them.
Faces yes, I never forget a face because I happen to be naturally
   observant
And always have been since I was a tiny kiddie
But names! – Oh dear! I'm quite hopeless.
I feel such a fool sometimes
I do honestly.

Irene Vanbrugh Memorial Matinee: The Epilogue*

Your Majesty, Ladies and Gentlemen.
A little while ago a lady died
A lady who, for many of us here
Epitomized the dignity and pride
Of our profession. Over fifty years
Have passed since young Miss Vanbrugh's quality
Was stamped indelibly upon the hearts
Of Londoners. During those changing years
We were most privileged, not only us
Her colleagues who so loved and honoured her
But you as well, you on the other side.
Perhaps you took for granted (as you should)
The lightness of her touch in comedy;
The note of hidden laughter in her voice;
The way she used her hands to illustrate
Some subtle implication. She could charge
An ordinary line with so much wit
That even critics thought the play was good!
They, too, took her for granted (as they should).
Then on the other hand, the other mask
The mask of tragedy; she could wear that
With such authority that even we,
Her fellow actors could perceive
Through her most accurate and sure technique
Her truth, which was her talent, shining clear.
Your Majesty, Ladies and Gentlemen,
A little while ago this lady died
Apparently, only apparently,
For even though the art that she adorned
Must in its essence be ephemeral,
Players of her integrity and grace

Can never die. Although we shall not hear
That lyrical, gay voice again, nor see
The personal inimitable smile
That she bestowed on us at curtain calls
The theatre that she loved will still go on
Enriched immeasurably by the years
She gave to it. This epilogue is but
A prelude to the future she endowed
With so much legend, so much memory
For all the young beginners who will learn
Their intricate and fascinating trade
And owe perhaps, some measure of their fame
To the undying magic of her name.

*A matinee to the memory of the actress Irene Vanbrugh was held on 6 November 1950. Noël contributed this Epilogue.

A Question of
Values

Christopher Marlowe or Francis Bacon
    The author of *Lear* remains unshaken
Willie Herbert or Mary Fitton
      What does it matter? The Sonnets were written.

MUSICAL

"Play, orchestra, play
Play something light and sweet and gay
For we must have music,
We must have music
To drive our fears away."

Tonight at 8.30

Tribute to Ivor Novello*

Dear Ivor. Here we are, your world of friends
The Theatre world, the world you so adored
Each of us in our hearts remembering
Some aspect of you, something we can hold
Untarnished and inviolate until
For us as well the final curtain falls.
For some of us your talent, charm and fame
The outward trappings of your brilliant life,
Were all we knew of you and all we'll miss.
But others, like myself, who loved you well
And knew you intimately, here we stand
Strangely bewildered, lost, incredulous,
That you, so suddenly, should go away,
Those of us here to-night who have performed
And sung your melodies and said your words
Professionally, carefully rehearsed
Have felt, I know, behind their actor's pride
In acting, a deep, personal dismay –
A heartache underlying every phrase.
The heartache will eventually fade
The passing years will be considerate,
But one thing Time will never quite erase
Is memory. None of us will forget,
However long we live, your quality;
Your warm and loving heart; your prodigal,
Unfailing generosity, and all
Your numberless, uncounted kindnesses.
I hope, my dear, that after a short while
There'll be no further sorrow, no more tears
We must remember only all the years
Of fun and laughter that we owe to you.

Mournfulness would be sorry recompense
For all the joy you gave us all, all the jokes
Your lovely sense of humour let us share.
Gay is the word for all our memories
Gay they shall be for ever and a day
And there's no greater tribute we can pay.

*The playwright and composer Ivor Novello died in 1951 having been a lifelong
friend of Noël's. This Tribute was written for a memorial performance held on
7 October 1951.

Opera Notes

I feel inclined to send a teeny-weeny
Admonishment to dear Signor Bellini
For having seriously tried to form a
Coherent opera from *Norma*.

I think we must face the fact that the *Carmen* by Bizet
Is no more Spanish than the Champs-Elysées.

Should I desire to be driven mad
I'd book a seat for *Herodiade*
Which, although it's by Massenet who wrote *Manon*
Is really not a good thing to plan on
And gives me, by and large, more claust-
rophobia than *Faust*.

I often say, for which opera lovers attack me,
That if I were a soprano I'd let them sack me
Before I'd sing *Lakme*.

Nobody could bear to read a
Detailed synopsis of *Aida*
And we all know the plot of *La Gioconda*
Is apt to wander.
But neither of these so arch and sticky is
As *Gianni Schicchi* is.

Though Wolfgang Mozart wrote *The Magic Flute* he
Alas, alas, composed *Così Fan Tutte*
The roguishness of which is piu piu male
Than *Don Pasquale*
But then poor Donizetti
Was likewise not
Too hot
At choosing libretti.

Then there are those *Rosenkavaliers* and *Fledermauses*
Written by all those Strausses
Which play to crowded houses
And, to me, are louses.
There couldn't be a sillier story
Than *Il Trovatore*
And yet, and yet, and yet Oh
Just think of the libretto
Of *Rigoletto!*
Both of these were set to music by Verdi
How dared he?
On the other hand we must admit that *Thais*
Is more concäis
And fairly näis

We must also admit that every Victorian hurdy-gurdy
Owes a deep debt of gratitude to Guiseppe Verdi.

WAR . . . AND
PEACE

WAR

"Every Blitz
Your resistance
Toughening
From the Ritz
To the Anchor and Crown,
Nothing ever could override
The pride of London Town."

London Pride

Personal Note

Creative impulse whether fine, austere,
Or light in texture; great in scope, or small,
Owes to its owner, if it's true at all
Some moments of release in this dark year.

Feeling my spirit battered, bludgeoned, sore,
All my ideas so pale, oppressed by doom,
Like frightened children in a burning room
Scurrying round and round to find the door,

Feeling the world so shadowed, and the time,
Essential to clear processes of thought,
So much accelerated, I have sought
Relief by those excursions into rhyme.

I must confess I have no mind just now
To write gay Operettes, Reviews or Plays
Nor leisure, for these swiftly moving days
Have set my hand to quite a different plough.

And what a different plough! An office desk;
Large trays marked 'In' and 'Out'; a daily load
Of turgid memoranda, and a code
That lends itself too glibly to burlesque.

From this new language that I have to learn,
From these dull documents, these dry reports,
From this dank verbiage, from these cohorts
Of qualifying adjectives, I turn –

135

And for a while, perhaps a few brief hours,
My mental muscles gratefully expand
To form these unimportant verses and
Like Ferdinand the Bull, I sniff the flowers.

Lie in the Dark
and Listen

Lie in the dark and listen,
It's clear tonight so they're flying high
Hundreds of them, thousands perhaps,
Riding the icy, moonlight sky.
Men, material, bombs and maps
Altimeters and guns and charts
Coffee, sandwiches, fleece-lined boots
Bones and muscles and minds and hearts
English saplings with English roots
Deep in the earth they've left below
Lie in the dark and let them go
Lie in the dark and listen.

Lie in the dark and listen
They're going over in waves and waves
High above villages, hills and streams
Country churches and little graves
And little citizen's worried dreams.
Very soon they'll have reached the sea
And far below them will lie the bays
And coves and sands where they used to be
Taken for summer holidays.
Lie in the dark and let them go
Lie in the dark and listen.

Lie in the dark and listen
City magnates and steel contractors,
Factory workers and politicians
Soft, hysterical little actors
Ballet dancers, 'Reserved' musicians,
Safe in your warm, civilian beds.
Count your profits and count your sheep
Life is flying above your heads
Just turn over and try to sleep.
Lie in the dark and let them go
Theirs is a world you'll never know
Lie in the dark and listen.

We Must Have a
Speech from a Minister

We must have a speech from a minister,
It's what we've been trained to expect.
We're faced with defeat and despair and disaster,
We couldn't be losing our Colonies faster,
We know that we haven't the guns to defend
The 'Mermaid' at Rye, or the pier at Southend;
You have no idea how we've grown to depend
In hours of crisis
On whacking great slices
Of verbal evasion and dissimulation,
A nice Governmental appeal to the Nation
We'd listen to gladly with awe and respect,
We know that the moment is sinister
And what we've been earnestly trained to expect,
When such moments we reach,
Is a lovely long speech,
(Not a comment or chat
About this, about that)
But a really long speech,
An extremely long speech,
An ambiguous speech from a minister.

We must have a speech from a minister,
We don't mind a bit who it is
As long as we get that drab lack of conviction,
That dismal, self-conscious, inadequate diction.
We find Mr. Churchill a trifle uncouth;
His ill-repressed passion for telling the truth.
His 'Eye for an Eye' and his 'Tooth for a Tooth'
Is violent, too snappy,
We'd be far more happy

With some old Appeaser's inert peroration,
We'd give ourselves up to complete resignation,
Refusing to worry or get in a frizz.
We know that the moment is sinister,
We've already said we don't mind who it is,
We'd fight on the beach
For a really long speach,
(Not a breezy address,
Or a postscript on Hess)
But a lovely long speech,
A supremely long speech,
An embarrassing speech from a minister.

Lines to
an American Officer

These lines are dedicated to a man
I met in Glasgow, an American.
He was an army officer, not old,
In the late twenties. If the truth were told
A great deal younger than he thought he was.
I mention this ironically because
After we'd had a drink or two he said
Something so naive, so foolish, that I fled.
This was December, nineteen forty-two.
He said: 'We're here to win the war for you!'

Now listen – I'm a Britisher.
I love America and know it well.
I know its fine tradition, much of its land
From California to Maine. I know the grand
Sweep of the Colorado mountains; the sweet smell
Of lilac in Connecticut; I close my eyes
And see the glittering pageant of New York
Blazing against the evening sky; I walk
In memory, along Park Avenue, over the rise
Before Grand Central station; then Broadway
Seared by the hard, uncompromising glare
Of noon, the crowded sidewalks of Times Square
So disenchanted by the light of day
With all the sky-signs dark, before the night
Brings back the magic. Or I can wait
High on a hill above the Golden Gate
To see a ship pass through. I could recite

All the States of the Union, or at least
I think I could. I've seen the Autumn flame
Along the upper Hudson. I could reclaim
So many memories. I know the East,
The West, the Middle West, the North, the wide,
Flat plains of Iowa; the South in Spring,
The painted streets of Charleston echoing
Past elegance. I know with pride
The friendship of Americans, that clear, kind,
Motiveless hospitality; the warm,
Always surprising, always beguiling charm
Of being made to feel at home. I find,
And have found, all the times that I've returned,
This heartening friendliness. Now comes the war.
Not such a simple issue as before.
More than our patriotism is concerned
In this grim chaos. Everything we believe,
Everything we inherit, all our past
Yesterdays, to-days, to-morrows, cast
Into the holocaust. Do not deceive
Yourself. This is no opportunity
For showing off; no moment to behave
Arrogantly. Remember, all are brave
Who fight for Truth. Our hope is Unity.
Do not destroy this hope with shallow words.
The future of the world is in our hands
If we remain together. All the lands
That long for freedom; all the starving herds
Of tortured Europe look to us to raise
Them from their slavery. Don't undermine
The values of our conflict with a line,
An irritating, silly, boastful phrase!

Remember – I'm a Britisher.
I know my country's faults. Its rather slow
Superior assumptions; its aloof
Conviction of its destiny. The proof
Of its true quality also, I know,

142

This lies much deeper. When we stood alone,
Besieged for one long, agonising year,
The only bulwark in our hemisphere
Defying tyranny. In this was shown
The temper of our people. Don't forget
That lonely year. It isn't lease or lend,
Or armaments, or speeches that defend
The principles of living. There's no debt
Between your land and mine except that year.
All our past errors, all our omissive sins
Must be wiped out. This war no nation wins.
Remember that when you are over here.
Also remember that the future peace
For which we're fighting cannot be maintained
By wasting time contesting who has gained
Which victory. When all the battles cease
Then, if we've learned by mutual endurance,
By dangers shared, by fighting side by side,
To understand each other, then we'll forge a pride,
Not in ourselves, but in our joint assurance
To the whole world, when all the carnage ends,
That men can still be free and still be friends.

Lines to a Remote Garrison

When, at long last, this desolate and bloody war is won
And the men who fought it, lived in it and died in it
Have done their job as best they could in rain and sand and sun
Without much time to take excessive pride in it
When these heroic soldiers, sailors, airmen and marines
Are written of in poems, plays and stories
The emphasis will be upon the more dramatic scenes
The sacrifices, tragedies and glories
That this will be, that this should be is right and just and true
A very fitting Anglo-Saxon attitude
But there are many fighting men stuck in one place like you
To whom we owe a lasting debt of gratitude
It isn't only action, fire and flame that win a War
It isn't all invading and attacking
It takes a lot of guts to keep your spirits up to par
When you know that the essential thing is lacking
The battle area is wide, it stretches round the world
There are islands, deserts, mountains, rocks and crannies
There are many places where the flag of fredom's still unfurled
Where so many men are sitting on their fannies
And they, like you, just sit and wait, eternally prepared
Manoeuvering – parading, doing courses
They haven't even anything of which they need be scared
Except the nightly program for the Forces!
They write long letters home and then re-write the things they
    wrote
Remembering the sharp eye of the censor
And sometimes they are stationed in a place that's so remote
That they never even get a smell of E.N.S.A.

Try to remember now and then when browned off and depressed
And when you're feeling definitely out of it
That everybody knows that when it does come to the test
That you're ready and you're steady and you're primed to do your
    best
And that no-one's ever had the slightest doubt of it.

I've Just Come Out From England

I've just come out from England, and I feel
Foolishly empty-handed, for I bring
Nothing to you but words. But even so,
Even mere words can now and then reveal
A little truth. I know, or think I know,
If only I had had the chance to go
To all your homes and talk to all your mothers,
Wives and sweethearts, sisters, fathers, brothers;
What they'd have said and wanted me to say.
Those messages, unspoken, wouldn't ring
With sentimental pride, they'd be restrained.
We British hate to give ourselves away,
All our traditions having firmly trained
Our minds to shun emotional display.
Our people always under-state with such
Determined nonchalance, whether it's praise
Or blame; anger or joy or woe,
However moved they are, or may have been,
They'll very very seldom tell you so.
But still, beneath the crust we feel as much,
If not a great deal more than those who sob
And weep and laugh too easily. My job,
Being a writer, is to read between
The lines that others write; to look behind
The words they string together and to find
The right translation, the right paraphrase
Of what they feel rather than what they say.

What they would say, those patient people who
So very lovingly belong to you,
Would be extremely simple, almost off-hand:
'Give Jack my love' 'Tell Bert to come home soon'
'Tell Fred Aunt Nora's gone, he'll understand'
'Tell Jimmy everybody's doing fine'
'Give George our love and tell him Stan's had leave
And Elsie's doing war-work nine till nine'
'Tell Billy that last Sunday afternoon
We saw a newsreel and we recognised
Him on a tank – we weren't half surprised . . . '
It wouldn't take a genius to perceive
What lies behind those ordinary phrases
But on my own responsibility
I'd like to tell you what I know to be
Deep in the hearts of all of us in Britain.
The war's been long, it's had its tragic phases,
Its black defeats, its violent ups and downs,
But now, in all the villages and towns
That lie between Land's End and John-o'-Groats,
Hope is restored, new faith in victory,
New faith in more than victory, new pride
In something that deep down we always knew,
Thus, at long last, through you and all you've done,
We have been proved again. Much will be written
In future years. Historians will spew
Long treatises on your triumphant story,
They'll rightly praise your gallantry and glory
And probably embarrass you a lot.
They'll make exhaustive military notes,
Argue each battle fought, from every side,
But maybe they'll forget to say the one
Important thing. Four simple words are not
Unlikely, midst so much, to get mislaid:
For once I feel I need not be afraid
Of being sentimental. I can say
What those at home, who miss you and have such
Deep pride in you, would wish me to convey,
In four short words – note the true English touch –
The words are simply: 'Thank you very much.'

147

'Happy New Year'

'Happy New Year' the fifth year of the war.
'To Victory' – 'To Nineteen Forty-four'
'To all our fighting men' 'To their release
From carnage' – 'To a world at last at peace'
These were the words we said. The glib, confused
Hopelessly hopeful phrases that we used.
Then we had more champagne – somebody sang
Supper was served – outside we heard a gang
Of revellers gaily carousing by
Blowing their foolish squeakers at the sky.
'Happy New Year' – Happy New Year for whom?
How many people in that scented room?
How many people in that drunken crew
Squealing and swaying down Fifth Avenue
Thought for a moment; felt the faintest doubt;
Wondered what they were being gay about?
Here in New York, with shrill conviviality
Toasting their lack of contact with reality.
Lifting my glass, I sadly bowed my head
Silently to congratulate the Dead.

PEACE

"Sigh no more, sigh no more.
Grey clouds of sorrow fill the sky no more."

Sigh No More

The Battle of Britain Dinner, New York, 1963

I have been to the 'Battle of Britain' dinner.
Held at the Hotel Shelbourne on 37th street and Lexington
And there they were, a few survivors
Of that long dead victory
And there they were too, the non-survivors
Somewhere in the air above us,
Or at any rate in our hearts
The young men who died, humorously, gaily, making jokes
Until the moment when swift blazing death annihilated them.
And there we were, raising our glasses to them
Drinking to their intolerable gallantry
And trying to make believe that their sacrifice
Was worth while
Perhaps it was worth while for them, but not for us.
They flew out of life triumphant, leaving us to see
The ideal that they died for humiliated and betrayed
Even more than it had been betrayed at Munich
To those conceited, foolish, frightened old men.
To-day in our country it is the young men who are frightened
They write shrill plays about defeat and are hailed as progressive
They disdain our great heritage. They have been labelled by their
    dull
Facile contemporaries as 'Angry Young Men'
But they are not angry, merely scared and ignorant,
Many of them are not even English
But humourless refugees from alien lands
Seeking protection in our English sanity
And spitting on the valiant centuries
That made the sanity possible.

These clever ones, these terrified young men
Who so fear extinction and the atom bomb
Have little in common with the men we were remembering to-
    night.
Whatever fears they had remained unspoken. They flew daily and
    nightly into the sky
Heavily outnumbered by the enemy and saved us for one valedictory
    year
Gave us one last great chance
To prove to a bemused and muddled world
Our basic quality. All that was done.
The year was lived alone and then
Conveniently forgotten and dismissed
Except for just one night in each long year.
We raised our glasses sentimentally
An Air Vice-Marshal made a brief, appropriate speech
And then we chatted a little, oppressed by anti-climax
And finally said good-night and went our ways.

Letter from the Seaside 1880

Dearest Mama
Here we all are
Safely arrived, with everything unpacked
Excepting the pilgrim basket and Laura's box
Which we are leaving until after tea
Because we want to go down to the sea
And look for seaweed and limpets on the rocks
And walk along the sands towards the caves
On the very edge of the waves.
We had, on the whole, a most agreeable journey
But for the fact
That poor Belinda
(Everything always happens to Belinda)
Got something in her eye, a piece of cinder.
You can imagine the relief
When Nanny cleverly managed to extract
The sharp invader with her handkerchief.
The name of our landlady is Mrs Gurney.

Later. After tea.
Dearest Mama how glad, how proud you'll be
Arnold has paddled twice!
At first he was frightened and sat down and cried
On that hard kind of sand that's wrinkled by the tide
Until Nanny produced a piece of coconut-ice
Which we had bought in a shop on the Parade.

Soon his tears were dried, then suddenly, unafraid
Away he went, brave as a lion
Upheld on each side
By Belinda and Bryan
A tiny epitome of 'Hearts and Oak'
Kicking the little wavelets as they broke!

For tea we had shrimps and cake and bread and butter
And they were pink, the shrimps I mean, bright pink
Can you imagine what Aunt Knox would think?
Can you not hear the prophecies she'd utter?
Her disapproving tone, her fearful warning
That we should all be dead before the morning!

These lodgings are very comfortable
Though we haven't yet tried the beds
Belinda and Laura are in the front
With a lithograph of Cain and Abel
And 'The Light of the World' by Holman Hunt
Hanging above their heads.

Nanny's bedroom, which Arnold shares
Is across the landing and down three stairs.
Bryan and I have two small rooms
On the very topmost floor.
His is in front and mine's at the back
And a picture faces my door
Which someone cut out of an almanac
A picture of dashing young Hussars
Galloping off to war.
On the chest of drawers by the looking-glass
There is – Imagine! – dried pampas-grass
Waving its fusty, dusty plumes
From a yellow Japanese vase.
But I can see over the sleeping town
To the curving line of the Sussex Down
And the sky and the moon and the stars.

Dearest Mama
Here we all are
Missing you so and wishing you could share
This pleasant gaslit room and the bracing air
And the prospect of to-morrow
For we are going on a picnic to a little bay
Beyond the lighthouse, several miles away.
Nanny has arranged with a Mr Wells
To drive us in his wagonette
(Unless, of course, it's wet)
And Mrs Gurney says that we can borrow
A wicker basket that she has, with handles,
In which to put the shells
And coloured pebbles that we hope to find on the deserted shore
Because, it seems, this particular beach
Is out of reach
Of ordinary visitors and is therefore lonely
Oh dearest Mama – if only – if only
You could be here with us. Now I must end
This untidy, rambling letter
For Nanny has come in with our bedroom candles.
We all of us pray Papa will soon be better
And that to-morrow's weather will be fine.
Your loving and devoted – Caroline.

TRAVEL ... AND
TRAVELLERS

————————————————————

TRAVEL

"The world is wide, and when my day is done
I shall at least have travelled free,
Led by this wanderlust that turns my eyes to far horizons."

I Travel Alone

On Leaving England
for the First Time

When I left England first, long years ago,
I looked back at the swiftly fading shore
And suddenly, quite without warning, knew
That I was sad at leaving. It is true
That I was on a holiday, no war
Was dragging me abroad, but even so!
How strange it was. How strange it is, this strong,
Deep-rooted feeling, for one's native land.
When is it born? Why should it come to flower
So inconveniently just at the hour
Of parting? I have grown to understand
In later years, after so many long,
Far journeyings. But on that distant day
When first I felt that unexpected, gentle
Tug at my heart, I tried to keep at bay
Such foolishness and, as I turned away,
Laughed at myself for being sentimental.

P. & O. 1930

The siren hoots three times its final warning
The first one long, the second two much shorter.
The passengers at the rail are suddenly stunned
Staring disconsolately at the Shanghai Bund
As the widening gulf of yellow river water
ᴗetween the ship and the shore
Presses it back upon its usual day
Painted kites fly in the windy morning,
The ceaseless bustle and the ceaseless noise,
The clanking trams, the cries of rickshaw boys
Grow faint. But long before
The black and khaki ship is under way
The aggressive bugles bray
Announcing 'Tiffin', while the passengers
Obedient and docile
Regardless of where he or she prefers
To sit, politely file
Like gentle horses entering their stables
To their appointed places at the tables.

Lines of chairs on the promenade deck,
Smell of engine room rising through hatches,
Mrs Blake, with a sunburnt neck,
Organizing Shuffleboard matches,
Missionaries with pale, kind eyes,
Drained of colour by savage skies,
Strumming militantly glum
Hymns on a harmonium.

Flying fish from the bow waves skittering,
Mrs Frobisher's endless tittering
And at night the great stars glittering.

Bugles blowing, deafening, instant,
The Governor's Lady amiable but distant,
Returning home for six months' leave
A necessary, all too brief reprieve
From State Receptions, Women's Federations,
Official visits to remote plantations,
From garden-parties under alien trees
And mocking, inefficient A.D.C.s.
Again the bugle's unrelenting blast,
Brown-sailed junks and sampans sailing past,
Clanging of ship's bells signalling the Watches,
Poor Mrs Vining's unbecoming blotches;
All her own fault, when all is said and done,
For sleeping on the boat-deck in the sun.
Mrs Ashpole, tremulously eager,
To pour out the minutiae of her meagre
Unreflective, imperceptive mind.
Major Morpeth, coarse and unrefined,
Mrs Morpeth, timid and retiring,
Both their daughters earnestly perspiring.
Colonel Wintringham, supreme at sports,
Tremendous knees beneath tremendous shorts,
Tremendous hands, tremendous calves and thighs
And small, submissive, vulnerable eyes.
Soup and water-biscuits at eleven,
Scampering of children over seven,
A fenced-in pen for children under five,
A frail old woman more dead than alive
Uninterested, withdrawn from social dramas,
Patiently tended by two Chinese Amahs.

Flying fish from the bow waves skittering,
Mrs Frobisher's endless tittering
And at night the great stars glittering.

In Hong Kong, Mrs Ashpole
Had an alarming experience
Which, without reticence,
After the ship had sailed again
She recounted in the saloon.
It appeared that she had lunched
At the Peninsular Hotel
(Which she knew well)
In Kowloon
And that later,
Crossing the harbour in the ferry
An American in a tussore suit said a very
Unpleasant word.
At first she imagined that she hadn't heard
Correctly
And said politely, circumspectly
'I beg your pardon'
Whereupon he lewdly winked his eye
And, believe it or not,
Actually pinched her thigh!
Apparently she practically fainted
And if the ferry hadn't happened to reach the landing
At that very moment
She didn't know what she'd have done.
At all events she left him standing
And went off at a run
Feeling humiliated
And, you know, sort of tainted!
Fortunately she remembered
That she kept handy
In her bag
A tiny flask of brandy
From which she felt compelled to take a nip
In the rickshaw on the way back to the ship.

The ship arrived at dawn in Singapore
But in the city day had long begun
The wider streets were bland and empty still
But shops, beneath the flaking green arcades,
Blazed the shrill colours of their merchandise,

164

Dark rain clouds, harassed by the quickening light
Moved off across the flat metallic sea
And crouched upon the far horizon's edge
Like trained but savage circus animals
Awaiting sullenly their next performance.
Colonel Wintringham, in spotless drill,
Snuffing the air like an escaping prisoner,
Stepped firmly from the gangway to the dock
And strode, epitome of just authority,
Through raucous crowds of hotel porters, priests,
Beggars, vendors of bright, unlikely fruits,
Sellers of silks and cottons, ornaments,
Tortoise-shell and oriental beads
And, hailing a rickshaw boy in brisk Malay,
Settled himself at ease and bowled away.

         Superficially like the sailor
         With a wife in every port
         Colonel Wintringham could depend
         On finding an understanding friend
         From Cape Town to Venezuela
         Of a rather special sort.
         The ship didn't sail till seven
         And desire, like a rising stream,
         Flooded Colonel Wintringham's kind,
         Unregenerate, private mind.
         And Oh for the secret heaven!
         And Oh for the secret dream!

The siren hoots three times its final warning
The first one long, the second two much shorter,
Passengers at the deck rail wave to friends
New life begins before the old life ends.
The lights reflected in the harbour water
Like yellow serpents twist
And Colonel Wintringham stands
As spick and span as, in the far-off morning,
He'd set forth with his demons clamouring
His body tense, his pulses hammering,
To his peculiar tryst.

Now, only the faintest tremor of his hands
Betrays his recent, ardent sarabands.
Whistles are blown, the bugles shrilly bray again
The harbour sounds fade in the freshening breeze,
The crowded dock begins to slide away again.
Impassively the Colonel hears and sees
The last 'Good-byes', the coloured streamers fluttering
And two pale nuns interminably muttering.

Mrs Macomber in her steamer chair
Closed her tired eyes against the burning sky
And looked back over eighty-seven years
To when she was a child in Winchelsea.
The house was long and low, or so it seemed,
There was a sunken garden with small paths
Winding among bright flower beds, and beyond
The lichened red-brick wall, an old, old tree
Stretched out its branches to the distant sea.
An orchard lay behind the house and Spring
Scattered its shaded grass with primroses
Later the catkins and the bluebells came
And there was a wooden swing.
The memories of different years and different flowers
In different gardens flowed into her mind . . .

     Five planter's children played Hide and Seek
     Ran shrieking back and forth along the deck
     White-coated stewards swooped between the chairs
     Delivering bowls of soup and sandwiches.

But Mrs Macomber stayed behind her eyes
Removed from all disturbance, quiet and still
Remembering other voyages long ago,
Remembering the walled city of Pekin
When first she went to live there as a bride;
The lacquered temples on the Western hills,
The early morning rides; watching the dawn
Staining with light the terra-cotta plains;
The Empress Dowager, sharp and malign,
Monstrously attired in Highland tartan
Receiving Ministers at four a.m.

166

And Mac, beloved Mac, in full court dress
Cursing Imperial capriciousness.
And then the children growing up and leaving
To cross these same warm seas to go to school;
The loving, dying, marrying and grieving,
The happy moments and the empty hours
Waiting for the news from England, waiting alone
In that blank echoing house in Wei Hai Wei.
Then suddenly, quite suddenly, when Mac was killed,
Becoming aware that youth and middle-age
Had slipped into the past and were no more
And that there was little to look foward to
Beyond the changing seasons and the cold,
Niggardly compensations of the old
Mrs Macomber in her steamer chair
Closing her eyes against the burning sky
Knew, without terror and without despair,
That the time had come for her to die.

Mrs Macomber was laid to rest at four forty-five p.m.
The ship reduced its speed and slowly, slowly came to a halt.
The missionaries provided a suitable Requiem
And a little grey cat ran out of a hatch which wasn't anyone's
    fault.
The Captain read the service which was mercifully brief.
The coffin slid into the water from under its covering flag
And one of the Chinese Amahs, assaulted by sudden grief,
Fumbled to find a handkerchief in a little beaded bag.
Mrs Frobisher summed it all up that afternoon at tea
'There's nothing more impressive' she said 'than a burial at sea.'

　　The ship pursues its course, the days go by
　　Romances bloom, tensions intensify.
　　Mrs Macgrath and Mrs Drage have words
　　Cawing and spluttering like angry birds
　　Until Mrs Drage, with mottled, scarlet neck
　　Utters a strangled cry and leaves the deck.
　　That dreadful girl in the revealing jumper
　　Who had to be sent home from Kuala Lumpur

Is found, inside a lifeboat after dinner
Recumbent in the arms of Major Skinner.
Amusements are relentlessly devised
A Deck Quoits tournament is organized,
Competitors are bidden to confab in
The sacred precincts of the Captain's cabin.
A dance is given, fancy dress 'de rigeur'
And Colonel Wintringham, his massive figure
Draped in a towel of enormous size
Coyly accepts the consolation prize.
The Deck Quoits tournament is fought and won
By Mr Frith and Mrs Cuthbertson.
The ship pursues its course, nights follow days,
The five-piece orchestra tirelessly plays
Selections from the classics, German lieder,
'Les Cloches de Corneville', 'Celeste Aida'
And, as a musical salute to Asia,
Extracts from *The Mikado* and *The Geisha*.

Colombo, viewed from the approaching ship
Looked, in the distance, like bright coloured stones
Flung onto emerald and cinnabar hills
Behind which, serried ranks of mountains stood
Some of them veiled in cloud and some quite clear
Sharply defined against the morning sky.
Mrs Frobisher, wearing shaded tones
Of pink and lavender, adorned with frills,
Emitting girlishly her usual trills
Of unprovoked amusement, stepped ashore
Escorted by the victorious Mr Frith
Who'd given Mrs Cuthbertson the slip
And, needing someone to go shopping with,
Had offered his services as cavalier.
Mrs Frobisher knew Colombo well
And, prior to lunch at the Galle Face Hotel
Led him immediately to a store
Where a be-turbaned, dark eyed Bengalese
Welcomed them with soft, obsequious sighs
And emptied from little chamois leather sacks

A scintillating, miscellaneous flood
Of zircons, amethysts, aquamarines,
Star sapphires, rubies pale as watered blood,
Opals, agates, cat's eyes, tourmalines
And cultured pearls as big as garden peas.
Poor Mr Frith stared glumly at the stacks
Of gems, so few of which he could afford,
And wished to God that he'd remained on board.
However, after arguing awhile,
Appraising each small stone from every angle,
The Bengalese, to Mr Frith's surprise,
Smiled with a patient, understanding smile
And finally agreed to compromise.
A set of tourmalines for Mrs Frith
(Later to be set into a bangle)
Eight zircons, carefully matched, later to be
Fashioned with cunning ingenuity
Into some studs and links for evening dress,
Not flashy, mind you, but discreetly sober.
Then Mr Frith, dazed by his own largesse,
Gave Mrs Frobisher an opal pin
(Quite safe because her birth month was October).
The whole lot, plus a garnet crucifix
The Bengalese obligingly threw in,
Cost Twenty-seven pounds, thirteen and six.

The Governor's Lady's steamer chair
Is set a little apart
And day after day she sits in it
And reads in it and knits in it
With a chiffon scarf to protect her hair
And loneliness in her heart.

She is sick of tropical greenery
And everything Asiatic
She is tired of lizards and parakeets,
Scarlet hibiscus and tom-tom beats
And her eyes are aching for scenery
That's a little less dramatic.

She seems immune from despairs and joys
Her bones are brittle with breeding.
It isn't easy to reconcile
Her unexpected, disarming smile
With the hard façade of her social poise
Which is definitely misleading.

She answers politely when addressed
Her coat has a Redfern label.
Inwardly timorous and shy
She goes through life with her head held high
And, indestructibly self-possessed,
Dines at the Captain's table.

The voyage continues, still the bugles blow,
Meal follows meal, the temperature below
Rises to quite unprecedented heights
Curbing the most voracious appetites.

Mrs Drage, as though felled by a truncheon
Faints at the Purser's table during luncheon.
Outside, the Indian Ocean, stretched like glass,
Beneath a carapace of burnished brass,
Heaves with a gentle, oily under-swell
And Mrs Vining, feeling far from well,
Suddenly gives a cry, clutches her head,
And runs precipitately to her bed.

But every evening, cold or hot,
Whether the sea is rough or not
Mr Burden, Mr Knapp
(The one that wears the yachting cap),
Mr Haggerty from Rangoon,
Travelling with Mr Witherspoon,
Bobby Green and 'Nutty' Boyle
(Agents, both, from Standard Oil)
Mr Randall, Harry Mott,
And tiny Mr Appendrodt
Come rain, come shine, come joy, come doom,
Assemble in the smoking-room.

These little men who travel far
How infinitely dull they are
You find them in the ships that ply
Between Manila and Shanghai,
From Tripoli to Port Sudan,
Shimonosaki to Fusan
You find them everywhere you go
And always in a P. and O.
These little men who travel far
Drinking forlornly at the bar
'This is my round' and then 'One more'
'Stop me if you've heard this before'
Each one endeavouring to cap
The story of the other chap.
From Trinidad to Panama,
From Brindisi to Zanzibar,
From Alexandria to Crete,
These lethal raconteurs compete.
The loudest laugh, the coarsest joke,
Each shouting down the last who spoke,
Each ego straining more and more.
Insensately to hold the floor.
The barman, with unsmiling eyes,
Smiles at such dismal vanities.
The smallest fish beneath the keel
With every fishy instinct feel
Each ancient pornographic quip
Stately descending through the ship
Until at last with one accord
They sink away, profoundly bored.
The little men who travel far
How sadly insecure they are.

A word must be said for Mrs Rhys-Cunningham
Who embarked on the ship at Bombay
Accompanied by the Viscount Harringford,
The Honourable Evan and Mrs Blair
And a little bird-like man called Ossie Blenkinsop
Who was the life and soul of the party
And made comments on everybody and everything
In a high-pitched, rather affected voice.

They had all been staying with some Maharajah
And Mrs Rhys-Cunningham and Mrs Blair
Appeared each night at dinner in different saris
Gossamer light, magenta, yellow and blue,
Threaded with gold and silver. Even the men
Wore tokens of their host's munificence;
Ossie had links like golden lotuses,
Blair and Lord Harringford, square signet rings
Of intricately carved chalcedony.
In the saloon they graced a separate table
Around which stewards hovered, thick as bees,
Tensed to anticipate their slightest wishes
Eagerly plying them with special dishes.
Lord Harringford had lustreless, blond hair
Smoothed back from a benign but narrow forehead
And, though his complexion was a trifle florid,
He had a certain charm, also of course
One felt he looked much better on a horse.
Unlike the Honourable Evan Blair
Who seemed, by Nature, wrought for an arm-chair.
Mrs Blair was definitely jolly,
Thick-set and freckled with a raucous laugh,
One saw her tramping Dartmoor with a collie
Or, in some stately hall festooned with holly,
Handing out Christmas presents to the staff.

            Mrs Rhys-Cunningham's widowed state
            Made little appeal for pity
            Her taste in clothes was immaculate,
            Her income, more than adequate
            And her face extremely pretty.

            Of weariness she showed no trace
            In spite of her Indian Odysseys
            Her figure was slim and moved with grace
            Along the deck's restricted space
            Like one of the minor goddesses.

She and her party remained aloof
Preoccupied and serene
From the *va-et-vient* and the warp and woof,
The daily recurring *Opéra Bouffe*
Of shipboard's defined routine.

So sure they were, so secure they were
So ineffably centrifugal
So set apart from the common weal,
Never in time for any meal
Disdainful of gong or bugle.

They failed to observe the looks of hate
The lips so cynically curved,
Tantalizingly intimate
They giggled and talked and stayed up late
Enclosed in their private world.

Between Bombay and the Gulf of Aden
An unexpected storm pounced in the night
And, seizing the ship like a ratting terrier,
Shook it and savaged it. The tranquil sea
As though bored by its own monotony
Rose up and, whipped by the shrieking wind,
Changed into ambulant, grey mountain peaks
Advancing endlessly, and in between
Their walls of grim implacability
Fell sickening valleys streaked with veins of foam.
The ship, reducing speed, received the first
Violent assault with shuddering acquiescence,
Pitching and tossing, rolling drunkenly,
Battered and bruised, sodden with flying spray,
She stubbornly proceeded on her way.
The cabins creaked and groaned: vases of flowers
Flew through the air as though endowed with wings,
Avalanches of books and toilet things
Tumbled onto the sleepers in their bunks
While, in the baggage room, enormous trunks
Rumbled and crashed with each vibrating roll.
Mrs Macgrath, who'd left her porthole open,
Woke with a scream to see her lamé dress

Swirling about like some strange jellyfish
Together with her stockings, shoes and stays.

Poor Mr Frith sustained a nasty graze
When the large plate of fruit he always kept
Handy beside his bunk, suddenly leapt
And struck him on the temple while he slept.
Colonel Wintringham, in a sarong
Which gave due freedom to his massive legs
And left his body bare, awoke to find
A broken bottle of green brilliantine
Clotting the matted hair upon his chest
Where it malignantly had come to rest.
Mrs Frobisher arose and dressed
Uttering little moans and staggering,
The cabin stifled her, it lurched and heaved
Flinging her to and fro like a rag doll.
When finally her object was achieved
She sank disconsolate on her bunk
Armed with lifebelt and two winter coats,
And waited to be conducted to the boats.
Meanwhile the Governor's Lady, unafraid,
Asked the night stewardess to call her maid,
All the next day the hurricane continued,
Screamed through the rigging, tore at the plunging masts,
Hatches were battened down, the deck doors guarded
By weary stewards, empowered to prevent
Foolhardly passengers with iron stomachs
From venturing out to photograph the sea.
In the saloon 'fiddles' encased the tables,
Ropes were stretched taut across the creaking decks,
Stewards and stewardesses with covered basins
Swayed doggedly along the corridors
Moving unflurried through familiar hells
Of retchings, groanings and incessant bells.
In the deserted lounge, in time for tea,
The five-piece orchestra, reduced to three,
Valiantly and to its undying glory
Obliged with *Tosca* and *Il Trovatore*.
In the late afternoon, capriciously,

The storm clouds parted on the starboard beam
Revealing a strip of blue, unflurried sky.

An hour later, in a blaze of sun
The ship still wallowed, but the storm was done.
The sun beats down on Aden. The port officials drip,
The dusty buildings sizzle in the heat,
The grimy, black coal barges crowd obscenely round the ship
Like gaping coffins on a metal sheet.
The town has few attractions: no shaded avenues,
No fascinating vistas to explore.
The passengers have only two alternatives to choose,
To suffocate on board or go ashore.
Those who decide the latter is the less repellent plan
From the point of view of culture, draw a blank,
For they find the arid town has little more to offer than
Two so-called mermaids in a dingy tank.
These strange, mis-shapen creatures, constricted and morose,
Hauled up long since in some bewildering net
Stare fishily, unseeingly, when visitors draw close,
Grateful at least, at least, for being wet.
Just before evening when the brazen sky begins to cool
The ship sails and the harbour fades from view
Astern, the wake, unwinding like white ribbon from a spool
Stretches and coils upon the deepening blue
And Aden, stumbling back against the night
Suddenly beautiful, sinks out of sight.

From either bank of the Suez Canal
The desert marches to the sky
And, on the interminable sand
Stretching away to the Promised Land
Lean, meditative Arabs stand
Watching the ship go by.
So narrow is the waterway
You feel that by stretching out an arm
You could touch the hovels of mud and clay
Or pick a date from a dusty palm.
On the other side, beyond the day,
Beyond the night, the Sahara spills,
Beyond immediate prophecy

175

So far as to challenge Infinity
Until it at last, at last gives way
To lakes and beginnings of hills,
And then the tropics where coloured birds
Swift in flight as a falling star
Swooping over lumbering elephant herds
And the fevered jungles of Africa.

At Port Said, Mr Frith and Mrs Frobisher
Who'd been inseparable since Colombo
Strolled in the evening through crowded streets,
Mrs Frobisher dressed to the nines
Looking about her eagerly for signs
Indicative of strange exotic vices
For which the unattractive little town
Had, quite inaccurately, won renown.
They sat outside a cafe eating ices
Badgered by beggars and by fortune-tellers
By urchins bearing trays of vivid sweets
By servile Oriental carpet-sellers
Whose voices fluctuated with their prices.
The 'Gully-Gully' merchant's mumbo-jumbo
Left them depressed and dully mystified.
They watched, with lassitude, the agile tricks
Vanishing coins, recurrent baby chicks,
All the impressive, boring sleight of hand
Which nobody could ever understand.
Later they rose, jostled by 'lesser breeds'
Deafened by mendicant, subservient whining
And saw Mrs Macgrath and Mrs Vining
Bargaining for synthetic amber beads.
Presently Colonel Wintringham went by
Striding with back erect and shoulders high
And, trotting purposefully by his side,
A picturesque but dubious Arab guide.
Mrs Rhys-Cunningham wandered through the crowd
Accompanied by Ossie and the Blairs
Who, when Mrs Frobisher politely bowed
Acknowledged her with vaguely puzzled stares.
A seedy man drew Mr Frith apart
And swiftly flashed before his startled gaze

A snapsnot of an ageing Syrian tart
Placidly naked, fastening her stays.
Later they tried to dissipate their gloom
With champagne cocktails in the smoking-room.

The Mediterranean welcomed the ship
And flattered her with promises
Of cleaner airs and fresher winds
And Europe drawing slowly closer.
Deck games were played with keener zest
And here and there fur coats appeared
And one dark night on the starboard side
Stromboli, spurting flame, defied
The gentle sea and the quiet sky.
Later the mountains of Sicily
Painted lavender shadows against
A blazing sunset of green and rose.
The Shuttleboard finals came and went
With Mrs Blake the ultimate winner.
The second prize went to Major Skinner
And the Captain gave a gala dinner.
After Marseilles the atmosphere on board
Altered perceptibly. In the saloon
Passengers, by mutual accord,
Tacitly moved from their allotted places,
Closed up the ranks, filled in the gaps, ignored
The hitherto stern protocol, and soon
Banished from memory the familiar faces
Of those who had so treacherously planned
To leave the ship and go home overland.
Europe slid by upon the starboard side
To port, Africa hid below the sea
Gibraltar rose impressive, dignified
Knowing no rising sun could ever set
On such a symbol of Imperial pride
On such invulnerable majesty.
That night, the Rock, an ebon silhouette
Through Colonel Wintringham's binoculars
Vanished at last among the swaying stars.

The Bay of Biscay, true to form
Behaved in its usual way
Greeting the ship with rain and storm
And gunmetal seas and spray.
Once more the cabins creaked and groaned
One more the wind through the rigging moaned
Like sinners on Judgement Day
The gale blew stronger and lashed the waves
Like an overseer with a whip
The rain blew level as music staves
From bow to stern of the ship.
Poor Mrs Vining, the sport of fate
Fell, embedding her upper plate
In the flesh of her lower lip.
But when the tempest had ceased to roar
And had muted its sullen arrogance
And the stubborn vessel at last forebore
To bow to the ocean's exigence
The clouds dispersed, the horizon cleared
Some pale, unconvincing stars appeared
And Mrs Cuthbertson swore she saw
A light on the coast of France.

Of course there was a ship's concert
There is always a ship's concert
Given ostensibly in aid of the Seamen's Fund
Given ostensibly to divert the passengers
But really given for several other reasons.
The Seamen's Fund, we know, accrued some benefit
The passengers, we know, are fairly diverted
But over and above and behind and below
These clear, unquestionable advantages
There are other issues, other implications.
The battle of straining egos for the light
For that sweet hour of temporary recognition,
There is also to be considered the Purser's pride
The raging hunger in him to be satisfied
Once, once at least in course of every voyage.
How can he carry on each day's routine
Pacify passengers, deal with small complaints
Keep a sharp, suave and understanding eye

On diverse temperaments, without some hope
Of one rich moment when subservience ends
And he at least can dominate a while
Those, who by wealth and rank and circumstance
Are classified as his superiors?
At the ship's concert he can rise
Clad in benign authority and speak
A few well chosen introductory phrases.
Later, like other deities, rise again
And make a longer, more imposing speech,
Thanking the artists, thanking the orchestra
Thanking the Captain for his gracious presence
Thanking the audience for their kind reception
Thanking the universe, the moon and stars
For this clear, golden opportunity
To stand, upholder of a worthy cause
And hear the sound of personal applause.

The concert started with 'Veronique'
Played excessively loudly
And when it came to 'Swing High, Swing Low'
Mrs Blake, in the second row,
Hummed the melody proudly.
Then a young man of strong physique
With the air of a swaggering rebel
Embarked to everyone's surprise
On 'Take a Pair of Sparkling Eyes'
In a voice that was almost treble.
Next came a girl from the Second Class
With spectacles and a fiddle
Who, unaware that she was tone deaf
Played Rubinstein's 'Melody in F'
And lost her place in the middle.
A table steward with lungs of brass
Bellowed a song of Devon
And Colonel Wintringham, drenched in sweat,
With Mrs Drage, sang an arch duet
Entitled 'The Keys of Heaven'.
A boy in a Javanese sarong
Made everyone rather restive
By executing a native dance

Which, whether on purpose or by chance,
Was definitely suggestive.
Turn followed turn, song followed song
Until all at last was ended
And the Purser's ears, crimson with praise,
Re-echoed the Governor's Lady's phrase
'It has all been simply splendid!'

England at last. At first only a smudge
A blue smudge on a windy blue-grey morning
High mackerel sky and spray, barely discernible
Splintering white against the sullen rocks,
The granite obstinacy of Land's End.
Seagulls appear, one perches in the rigging,
Its curved beak like a yellow scimitar.
Passengers crowd the rails, eager to catch
The first glimpse, after months and years away
Of their beloved and inalienable home.
This is a moment that must be remembered
Set in the heart and mind, branded upon
The retinas of tired English eyes,
Tired of violent colours, tired of glare
And heat and sand and jungles and bright birds.
Eyes that so often longingly have gazed
Through beaded curtains of torrential rain
To gentler rain falling on English woods,
Eyes that have stared nostalgically beyond
Flowers too vivid in the blazing light
To quieter flowers in herbaceous borders
Snapdragons, pinks, sweet-williams, lupins, phlox
And gawky, unexotic hollyhocks.
The ship draws near to the welcoming land
Houses are visible, cottages white and grey
Scramble down between low, forbidding cliffs
To crescent coves of shining golden sand
And twisted harbours filled with fishing boats
The Lizard, crouching among its little waves
Inspires Mrs Vining to recall
That, when she was a girl of seventeen
Together with two cousins and a friend
She got caught by the tide at Kynance Cove

And had to spend several hours upon a ledge
Wet and bedraggled, frightened and woebegone
Until the coastguards came and rescued them.
The ship, most courteously, drew nearer still
And steams along less than a mile from shore.
Falmouth, Veryan, Porthpean, St Austell Bay
Fowey, Looe, Polperro, all identified
By Mrs Vining's overwhelming pride
At being the only one on board who 'knew
Her Cornwall inside out and through and through'.

The Eddystone Lighthouse, slim and white
Like a pencil stuck in the blue,
Plymouth Hoe and Babbacombe Bay
Gaunt rocks changing from red to grey
Until the slow diminishing light
Banishes them from view.

No one on board can quite relax
Poor Mr Frith gets drunk
And Mrs Frobisher, bathed in tears,
Sits, surrounded by souvenirs
Each one of which she carefully packs
With her hopes, in her cabin trunk.

Colonel Wintringham cannot sleep
Barred are the gates of Slumberland
He cannot make up his mind between
His sister's cottage at Bushey Green
A trip to the continent on the cheap
Or a walking tour in Northumberland.

Inscrutable, disconsolate
Remote from understanding
Counting the dark hours as they pass
Wide awake in the Second Class
Mrs Macomber's Amahs wait
To be told where to go on landing.

How evil the mind's continued rage!
How cruel the heart that hardens!
Aware of this truth, with smiling face
And overflowing with Christian grace
Mrs Macgrath asks Mrs Drage
To tea in Ennismore Gardens.

Last-minute packing finished and done
The long and wearisome journey over
The Governor's Lady, standing apart,
With a sudden lifting of her heart
Sees, like sentinels in the sun,
The arrogant cliffs of Dover.

Kent on the one side, Essex on the other
And the wide Thames Estuary lying in between.
Oilers, tankers, cargo-ships and tug-boats,
The churning yellow paddles of *The Margate Queen*.
Cockneys on a holiday, sound of concertinas
Vying with the seagulls squawking in the breeze,
Houses, wharves and factories, grey beside the river,
Behind them, marshes and a few tall trees.
Delicately, shrewdly, the black-funnelled liner
Dark hull whitened by the salt sea spray
Picks her way with dignity among her lesser sisters
And steams up to Tilbury through the warm June day.

    This then is the end. The end of longing,
    The realized anticipatory dream,
    The lovely moment, still unspoiled and tremulous
    Still lighter than a bubble, gay with hope,
    Still free from anti-climax, before Time
    Itself has had the time to tarnish it.
    The image of homecoming still unmarred
    By little disappointments, small delays
    And sudden, inexplicable dismays.

    The siren hoots three times, three warning calls,
    The first one long, the second two much shorter.
    And into the turgid, swirling river water
    The anchor falls.

182

Bora Bora

The wild lagoon in which the island lies
Changes its colours with the changing skies
And, lovely beyond belief,
The dazzling surf upon the outer reef
Murmurs its lonely, timeless lullaby
Warning the heart perhaps that life is brief
Measured against the sea's eternity.

In the lagoon beneath the surface grow
Wild fantasies of coral; to and fro
And, lovely beyond all praise,
The vivid fish interminably gaze:
Rubies and emeralds, yellows, blues and mauves
Endlessly nibbling at the coral sprays
Endlessly flitting through the coral groves.

The coco-palms paint shadows on the sand
Shadows that dance a languid saraband
And, lovely indeed to see,
Above the scented frangipani tree
The mountain's silhouette against the moon
Who, as she saunters through Infinity
Traces a silver path on the lagoon.

Jamaica

Jamaica's an island surrounded by sea
(Like Corsica, Guam and Tasmania)
The tourist does not need to wear a topee
Or other macabre miscellanea.
Remember that this is a tropical place
Where violent hues are abundant
And bright coloured clothes with a bright yellow face
Look, frankly, a trifle redundant.
A simple ensemble of trousers and shirt
Becomes both the saint and the sinner
And if a head-waiter looks bitterly hurt
You *can* wear a jacket for dinner.

Jamaica's an island surrounded by sea
(It shares this distinction with Elba)
Its easy to order a goat fricassee
But madness to ask for Pêche Melba.
You'll find (to the best of this writer's belief)
That if you want rice you can get it
But visitors ordering mutton or beef
Will certainly live to regret it.
There's seldom a shortage of ackees and yams
Or lobsters, if anyone's caught them
But if you've a passion for imported hams
You'd bloody well better import them.

Jamaica's an island surrounded by sea
(It has this in common with Cuba)
Its national tunes, to a certain degree,
Are founded on Boop-boop-a-duba.

'Neath tropical palms under tropical skies
Where equally tropical stars are
The vocal Jamaicans betray no surprise
However off-key their guitars are.
The native Calypsos which seem to be based
On hot-air-conditioned reflexes
Conclusively prove that to people of taste
There's nothing so funny as sex is.

Jamaica's an island surrounded by sea
(Like Alderney, Guernsey and Sark are)
Its wise not to drive with exuberant glee
Where large barracuda and shark are.
The reefs are entrancing; the water is clear,
The colouring couldn't be dreamier
But one coral scratch and you may spend a year
In bed with acute septicemia
The leading hotels are extremely well run
The service both cheerful and dextrous
But even the blisters you get from the sun
Are firmly included as extras

Jamaica's an island surrounded by sea
(*Unlike* Ecuador or Guiana)
The tourist may not have a 'Fromage de Brie'
But always can have a banana.
He also can have, if he has enough cash,
A pleasantly rum-sodden liver
And cure his rheumatic complaints in a flash
By shooting himself at Milk river
In fact every tourist who visits these shores
Can thank his benevolent Maker
For taking time off from the rest of His chores
To fashion the Isle of Jamaica.

Oh Dear

Oh dear oh dear
What am I doing here
It's all so very queer
Oh dear oh dear oh dear!

Batavia's a bugger
A bastard and a sod
So I'm back on board the lugger
With a hey ho and bollocks ahoy
I'm back on board the lugger
Thank the sweet Lord God.

These verses may appear to some
A teeny bit obscene
I'm only writing them to test
This fartarsing machine.
I've put a brand new ribbon in
And oiled each bloody screw
I've cleaned each letter with a pin
Each fucking letter with a pin
And now I really *must* begin
Some dreary work to do
With a hey whack knackers aho
Some dreary work to do.

If lots of sticks and stones and bits of larva
Abruptly came cascading through the air
And bollocksed up the sunny isle of Java
I don't believe that I should really care.
If pestilence, by order of the Saviour

Exclusively descended on the Dutch
Killing these podgy bastards in Batavia
I don't think I should mind so *very* much.

Bali

As I mentioned this morning to Charlie,
There is far too much music in Bali.
And altho' as a place it's entrancing,
There is also a *thought* too much dancing.
It appears that each Balinese native
From the womb to the tomb is creative,
Fron sunrise till long after sundown,
Without getting nervy or rundown,
They sculpt and they paint and they practise their songs,
They run through their dances and bang on their gongs,
Each writhe and each wriggle,
Each glamorous giggle,
Each sinuous action,
Is timed to a fraction.
And altho' the results are quite charming,
If sometimes a trifle alarming!
And altho' all the 'Lovelies' and 'Pretties'
Unblushingly brandish their titties,
The whole thing's a little *too clever*
And there's *too much artistic endeavour*!

Forgive the above mentioned Charlie,
I had to rhyme *something* with Bali.

Canton Island

Accept this testimonial from one
Who's travelled far, who's travelled fairly wide
Who's sought for many an island in the sun
And breasted many a changing tropic tide
Who, in the varied course of his career,
Has journeyed North and South and West and East,
Sharing with pleasure, not unmixed with fear,
The diverse habitats of man and beast.
This testimonial need not be scorned,
Idly dismissed or casually ignored
Especially as he who writes was warned
That here on Canton Island he'd be bored.
Bored! On this self-sufficient coral reef?
Bored with this fascinating personnel?
Bored with the luxury beyond belief
Of this irrelevant and strange hotel?
Where every meal provides a different thrill
Of gay anticipation; where each dish,
No matter how it's listed on the bill,
Tastes doggedly of oranges or fish.
Where modern science has so deftly brought
Refrigeration to the finest art
That even a Red Snapper freshly caught
Smells unmistakably of apple tart!
Where all the bedrooms are equipped with showers
With, written on the faucets, Cold and Hot
So that the passengers can pass the hours
Endeavouring to find out which is what.
Where, when you find your bed has not been made,
Little avails your anger or your sorrow,
Swiftly you learn to let emotion fade

Then ring the bell and *wait* for a Chamorro.
(Chamorros! Children of the Southern Seas,
Natives of Guam, incapable of crime,
Uncertain, coy but striving hard to please
So vague, so blissfully unaware of time.
How they have guessed, these innocents abroad,
That service, in a Democratic State
Has in its nonchalance, its own reward?
They also serve who only ring and wait.)
Who could be bored when each new day brings forth
Some psychological or cosmic twist,
Rain from the West; a cyclone from the North;
A new bug for the Entomologist;
A Clipper zooming down out of the night,
Disgorging passengers of different sorts;
Elderly Bankers blinking at the light,
Ladies in strained, abbreviated shorts,
Fat men and thin men, quiet men and loud
Out of the sky they come to rest below
Then when they've fed and slept, unshaven, cowed,
At crack of dawn, into the sky they go.
What sort of man is he who on this dot;
This speck in the Pacific; this remote
Arena full of plot and counterplot,
Could not be interested – could fail to note
The vital dramas, comedies, burlesques.
The loves, the hates, the ceaseless interplay;
The posturings, the human arabesques
Performed interminably day by day?
Who, if he's human, would not almost swoon
With pleasure as he dives from off the dock
Into the limpid depths of the lagoon
And meets an eel advancing round a rock?
Where is the witless fool who could deny
The fun of swimming gently in the dark
And wondering if that which brushed his thigh
Was just a sting-ray or a six foot shark?
The man who could be bored in this strange place.
The man unable to appreciate
The anguished look on everybody's face
When told the North-bound Clipper *isn't* late.

190

The man too unreceptive and too slow
To be responsive to the vibrant beat,
The pulse, the Life-Force, throbbing just below
The surface of this coral bound retreat,
Dear God that man I would not care to know!
Dear God that man I would not wish to meet!

Malta

The Isle of Malta lies at ease
Secure in old tradition,
Lapped by translucent azure seas
And social competition.
That service spirit dominates
All shabby habitations,
Controlling fears and loves and hates
And marital relations.
The visitor who is unused
To dealing with officials.
Will find his mother tongue reduced
To orgies of initials.
If Captain D is asked to T
To give himself more leisure
He signals W.M.P.
Which means 'Without much pleasure.'

Souvenir

In memory of a charming trip
On board a dull but noble ship
In memory of endless games
And scores of unrelated names
Including that of Doctor Wence
Who first discovered flatulence
Also the famous Elmer Hale
Who pitched a ball eight times for Yale
Without forgetting Witzenback
That hero of the Harvard Track
Nor Mrs. Hiram J. Macfarr
Who wandered, nude, through Iowa
Under these clarion trumpets' din
Sometimes a lesser name crept in
Such as Napoleon Bonaparte
Or even Plato or Mozart
But men of such obscure repute
Were seldom passed without dispute
So we returned with great relief
To Senator Augustus Spief
To Ada Chubb and Wendel Green
(The first to cauterise the spleen)
To Ethan Beck and General Bight
And Mabel Macnamara Wright
To Doctor Bowes, the insect man
Who perished in Afghanistan
Without a thought for Otto Kahn
Or Drian or Reynaldo Hahn.

Martinique

No Frenchman can forbear to speak
About the charms of Martinique
It seems it is a land of spice,
And sugar, and of all things nice
A veritable Paradise
Un endroit fantastique.

The Compagnie Translantique
Send lots of ships to Martinique
Because, they say, it's nicer far
Than many other places are
More glamorous than Zanzibar
Cleaner than Mozambique.

They also say it has more 'chic'
Than Tunis in the Nord d'Afrique
Possessing 'Plagues' with finer 'sable'
A climate 'Toujours admirable'
In fact, they say, it's 'Formidable'
This God-damned Martinique.

In praising this celestial Freak
They, one and all omit to speak
About its flat cathedral bells
Its indescribable hotels
The noisesome and disgusting smells
That make the Island reek.

Thoughts on Corsica

Descriptive

The Island of Corsica crouches at ease
Secure in its bloody tradition
Surrounded by changing, unamiable seas
And proudly immune from ambition.
The dogs and the chickens that scavenge the streets
The children that litter the ports
The goats, with their bulbous inelegant teats
And the insects of various sorts
The eagles that live on the furthermost peaks
And the natives that live in the vales
Appear to enjoy being battered for weeks
By the wild unaccountable gales.
When winds from the South, or the West, East, or North
Smear the skies with an ominous black
The Corsican fishermen bravely go forth
But seldom, if ever, come back.

Hotel Napoleon Bonaparte,
Ile Rousse

God bless the 'Messageries Maritimes'
For building this splendid hotel.
This modern, de luxe, and superb habitation
With passable food and sublime sanitation
This architect's vision in gay terra cotta
This dream, which if only the weather were hotter
And also if only the sea could be calm
Could soothe our frayed nerves with its infinite charm
This haven of rest with the mountains behind it
Would surely hold peace if we only could find it.

Advice from a Lady Who Has Visited
the Island Before

You really should see the Interior
It's honestly vastly superior
You won't leave the Island
Please don't leave the Island
Without having seen the Interior
The coast is quite gay
In a kind of way
But you must leave your stupid old yacht for a day
And really explore the Interior
Now what in the world could be drearier
Than *not* having seen the Interior?
Don't trouble to say in Ajaccio
Or Calvi or San Bonifacio
But just take a car
From wherever you are
And drive like a streak
Round each crag and each peak
And see the *real* Corsica
Genuine Corsica
(Hell-raising curves
But to Hell with your nerves!)
The coast is so dreadfully inferior
Compared with the *real* Interior.
You really *must* see the Interior.

Calvi

There is something very odd about the fishermen
In this picturesque and vivid little port
Though the muscles roll like boulders
Up and down their brawny shoulders
And their sea legs are conveniently short
There is something very odd about the fishermen
In this pretty and attractive little port.

What has miscarried here?
What has miscarried here?
Too many foreigners maybe have tarried here
Too many types from more decadent nations

Swaying their hips in San Tropez creations
Too many queer indeterminate creatures
Coaxing the sun to their nondescript features
What is occurring here?
What is occurring here?
Too many sibilant voices are purring here
Too many caps at provocative angles
Too many yachtsmen with platinum bangles
Too much extravagant shrill phraseology
Too much exuberant psycho-pathology.

There is something very strange about the fishermen
Though they're physically epitomes of grace
Though each child in the vicinity
Should prove their masculinity
And ardent procreation of the race
There is something *very* strange about the fishermen
In this charming and alluring little place.

The Bandit

A bandit inhabiting Corsica
Would never waste time on Divorsica
He'd kick the backside
Of his tedious bride
And gallop away on his horsica.

The Quinta Bates

No wand'ring Nomad hesitates
To patronize 'The Quinta Bates',
He finds it comfortable inside
And innocent of social pride.
He finds, on entering the gate
An atmospheric opiate.
The spirit of the place conserves
An anodyne for jangled nerves.
The water's hot, the beds are soft,
The meals are many a time and oft.
The flowers are sweet, the grass is green,
The toilet is austerely clean.
Which, in this ancient continent,
Occasions vast astonishment.
The food is more than 'luxe' enough,
The cook not only cooks enough
But builds each afternoon for tea
A model of gastronomy.
The furniture is nicely placed
And signifies a catholic taste.
The periods are slightly mixed,
Some are between and some betwixt.
All "touristas" who grumble fail
To comprehend this jumble sale.
The visitors are jumbled too
Here sit the Gentile and the Jew,
The Mining Engineer, the Don,
The Governess from Kensington,
The debutante from Sulphur Springs,
The Archaeologist who sings,
The Matron from the Middle West,

The Minister from Bucharest,
The brittle lady Novelist,
The arid Christian Scientist
Conversing with fraternal grace
In this remote maternal place.
And now I feel it would be nice
In praising this small Paradise,
To mention with an awe profound
The one who makes the wheels go round.
Her name is plainly Mrs. Bates,
A strange capricious whim of Fate's
To crown with such banality
So great a personality.
Her friends, who love the Quinta's frame,
Disdain this unromantic name,
And much prefer to call this dear,
Kind and enchanting person, 'Tia'
For 'Tia' is a word that trips
With more allurement from the lips
And can be used endearingly
With apposite felicity.
Tho' Tia is completely kind,
She has a keen and lively mind,
And when things seem too hard to bear,
She'll soundly and robustly swear
She's learned her life in Nature's School
And isn't anybody's fool.
Of every place I've been to yet
This I shall leave with most regret.
The Quinta is to blame for this
Peculiar metamorphosis.
I think the 'Carlton' and the 'Ritz',
Those Palaces at St. Moritz.
The 'Crillon' and the drab 'Meurice',
The 'Grandes Auberges' of Cannes and Nice
The 'Continental' in Belgrade,
And in Berlin 'The Esplanade',
And every hotel in the States
Should emulate the 'Quinta Bates'.

Tintagel

There's nothing much here but sea and sky
And cliffs and different birds;
Seamews, Cormorants, Cornish Chaffs;
King Arthur's Castle – (See photographs),
    A small golf course
    A lot of gorse
The sun goes down and the Seagulls cry
And it's lovely beyond all words.

There's nothing much here but sky and sea
Of varying blues and greys;
Primroses, if you care to look,
English nostalgia – (See Rupert Brooke)
    Soft, springy turf,
    The pounding surf.
There's nowhere else that I'd rather be,
And it's lovely beyond all praise.

Pleasure Cruise

Was this the ship that launched a thousand faces
Upon the bosom of the seven seas?
Was this the ship that bore to far off places
The scum of culture-keen democracies?

Viewed from the shore her spirit seems unwilted
Calmly she swings at anchor in the tide
Her funnels tilting as they always tilted
As though remembering her early pride.

Remembering, as some gay painted lady
Remembers hopeful days when life was young
Before expedience imposed the shady
Transactions she must now exist among.

Was this the ship that slid into the river
With such panache, with so much proud disdain
Greeting her love with an exultant shiver
Her bows anointed with the best champagne.

Was this the craft that won that record ribbon
Snatched from the straining might of larger ships
Surely the whole *Decline and Fall* of Gibbon
Couldn't describe so dismal an eclipse.

TRAVELLERS

"Why oh why do the wrong people travel
When the right people stay back home?"

Sail Away

Lines to
a Fellow Passenger

Mr. Samoa! Mr. Samoa!
Why are you such an unbearable boa?
Why do you turn first to one then the other
Crushing their spirits with 'Buddy and 'Brother'?
Have you no vestige of equable poise?
Why do you make such a desperate noise?
Why do you bawl so that Heaven could hear
Every event in your private career?
Why, when a group is quite harmlessly drinking,
Must you hold forth and annihilate thinking?
Why, without knowledge or verification,
Must you impart so much false information?
Why do you pander to small Japanese
Knowing they're eagerly planning to seize
All the possessions America holds,
All that the flag of your country enfolds?
Why were you nice to them? Was it because
Some inner need for unworthy applause
Spurred you to please them, to joke and to try
To prove you were really a 'regular guy'
Mr. Samoa! Mr. Samoa!
Note what I gracefully hinted befoa
Will you, for God's Sake, not be any moa
Such a pervasive and shattering boa?

Venice

Last Wednesday on the Piazza
Near San Marco's trecento Duomo
I observed una grassa ragazza
With a thin, Middle Western uomo.

He was swatting a piccola mosca
She was eating a chocolate gelato
While an orchestra played (from *La Tosca*)
A flat violin obbligato.

They stared at a dusty piccione
They spoke not a single parola
She ordered some Te con limone
He ordered an iced Coca-Cola.

And while the tramanto del sole
Set fire to the Grande Canale
She scribbled haphazard parole
On glazed cartoline postale.

Go to
Malta Little Girl

If your neck craves the matrimonial halter
Go to Malta
Little girl.
For the Fleet provides the answer to the maiden's prayer.
Foolish virgins don't despair
Set your cap at them
Have a slap at them
If you're firm enough
You can make them do their stuff.
If you've missed copulation in Gibralta
Go to Malta
Little girl.

Jeunesse Dorée

Ian Macnamara Wrexham-Smith
Always desired a friend to travel with
So it befell, one day on the Riviera
He ran across Guido di Falconiera
In fact the whole delightful thing began
Outside the Martinez Hotel in Cannes.

A mutually reminiscent chat.
A joke or two about some passing hat.
A swift, sure recognition of the truth
Concerning this or that sun-guilded youth
A few Bacardi cocktails and the pact
Of friendship was a gay, accomplished fact.

The early spring of nineteen thirty-one
Found them together basking in the sun
Wearing, in charming compliment to each,
Silk dressing-gowns, one yellow and one peach
Which, thanks to Lanvin's ingenuity,
Could be reversed and changed entirely.

The whole of July, nineteen thirty-two
They spent, in sailors trousers, in Corfu.
A little later in the self-same year
They both of them elected to appear,
At that strange party given by Hans Rosen.
In gaily coloured scarves and 'Lederhosen'.

The month of August, nineteen thirty-three
Saw them in pale blue shorts in Sicily.
In nineteen thirty-four and thirty-five

They took a long, and most enchanting drive
From Buda Pest, via Florence, to Bavaria
In linen shirts the shade of old wistaria.

In nineteen thirty-six the whole Aegean
Was ravished by the spectacle of Ian
And Guido, wearing Shiaparelli drawers
Closely akin to crêpe-de-chine plus fours.
This, tho' a quite innocuous caprice,
Hardly enhanced the glory that was Greece.

In nineteen thirty-seven all the Lido
Gazed with a certain vague dismay at Guido
And Ian as they minced along the plage
Wearing gold lockets which were far too large,
Closely knitted rompers, children's size,
With 'diamanté' anchors on their thighs.

Late in September, nineteen thirty-eight
Something that neither could anticipate
Sundered their gentle lives after the most
Delightful month on the Dalmatian Coast
During which time they both of them had been
Wearing, alas, an acid shade of green.

When they set out by steamer for Trieste
Guido (for once conventionally dressed)
Struck up a conversation with a Croat
Wearing a rather bizarre Gipsy's coat
And, when they finally arrived in Fiume,
Ian retired, in silence, to his room.

Later, a rather violent dispute
Spattered with tear-stains Guido's Tussore suit
Very much later still a further scena
Ended in sobs outside the Bar Marina
With the result that on the morning boat
Guido departed firmly, with the Croat.

So we must hope that Ian Wrexham-Smith
Finds someone more sincere to travel with.

Index of Titles